CRCE CENTRE FOR RESEARCH
INTO COMMUNIST ECONOMIES

Poland :
Stagnation, Collapse or Growth ?

A Report by an Independent Group of Economists in Poland

Preface
Andrzej Brzeski

Comment
Jacek Rostowski

£4.50

THE STATE OF
COMMUNIST ECONOMIES 3

THE STATE OF COMMUNIST ECONOMIES

The political and economic systems of East European communist countries are breaking down. Less is heard about other communist countries in the Third World; but while it is important not to overlook them, the centre of communist ideology remains in Eastern Europe and the rest are likely to follow a similar destiny.

Because of the crisis in Eastern Europe, it can no longer be deemed sufficient to follow these developments passively. Research must identify the reasons for failure and examine alternative policies that offer solutions for present problems.

To judge the success of policy by reference to the spread of prosperity and freedom involves a value judgement which can hardly be avoided. Any policy must be evaluated by reference to stated criteria and it is natural to compare results with those attained in liberal-democratic countries. Such aims would not be disputed even by the leaders of communist countries, although they take for granted that prosperity and freedom can be achieved only if the Communist Party is in power. Probing this claim should be a central concern of the Centre's research with a view to exploring alternative policies that could be made acceptable to the population, including communists themselves.

Our hope is that by examining solutions for problems of communist countries we would not only help improve life there, but would contribute to the extension of detente from cultural and business affairs to ideology so as to mitigate political confrontation.

THE RESEARCH CENTRE

To organise research along these lines the Centre for Research into Communist Economies was founded at the end of 1983 with the status of a charitable educational trust. It is initially relying on mainly outside collaborators with the later possibility of building up a small staff. It is financed by contributions and subscriptions.

The Centre has made an early start in commissioning outside experts, publishing their findings, and making them available to organisations with access to the public in Eastern Europe and elsewhere under communism, including radio stations and publishing houses in national languages. To facilitate research the Centre will organise symposia or seminars on particular aspects of communism, on groups of countries, or on individual economies. It will hope to invite experts to London for consultations and to sponsor visits to communist countries where appropriate in pursuit of specific projects.

The Centre has a Board of Trustees responsible for general and financial supervision, and an academic Advisory Council to supervise publications. The management of the Centre is in the hands of the General Director.

Poland:
Stagnation, Collapse or Growth?

A Report by an Independent Group of Economists in Poland

Preface

Andrzej Brzeski

Comment

Jacek Rostowski

Published by
THE CENTRE FOR RESEARCH INTO
COMMUNIST ECONOMIES
1988

Poland:
Stagnation, Collapse
or Growth?

First published in January 1988
by
The Centre for Research into Communist Economies
c/o Lord North Street, London SW1P 3LB

© The Centre for Research into Communist Economies, 1988

British Library Cataloguing in Publication Data

Poland: stagnation, collapse or growth?:
   a report by an independent group of economists
   in Poland. — (The State of communist economies,
   ISSN 0950-026X; 3).
   1.   Poland — Economic conditions — 1945-
   I.   Centre for Research into Communist Economies II. Series
   330.9438'055 HC337.P7

   ISBN 0-948027-08-8

Printed in Great Britain by
Pika Print Limited, Genotin Road, Enfield, Middx. EN1 2AA

Contents

Foreword

The communist-ruled economies are performing so indifferently that, one after another, their leaders are exhibiting, not only great concern but also a grudging readiness to try new ideas. This development is all to the good, because the problems of the communist economies cannot be resolved without much open-mindedness.

The Polish referendum of 29th November 1987 points to another requirement for successful change, namely the population must be involved. For real involvement it is not sufficient that the populations should be consulted on the course to be taken, but that it understands the causes of failure and is given an active role in overcoming it. Such a role implies acceptance by the authorities that people are sufficiently mature to put forward their own suggestions, and that competition of ideas is the way forward in politics as it is in science.

Today, it is increasingly possible to assert that the economy of no country can be run from one centre, as was widely believed possible 40 years ago. It will, therefore, become widely accepted that people must be given the right to look after themselves and to act on their own initiative whenever they spot new openings. Only then may prosperity return to severely-tried populations who no longer accept temporary hardships except as a starting point for better times. Some encouragement can be drawn from the transformation of Germany under Erhard after 1948, although what has to be overcome in communist countries is not wartime destruction but the even more insidious economic distortion and disruption.[1]

Like previous CRCE publications, this Paper is offered as a contribution to the discussion of how to emancipate the citizens of communist countries, rulers no less than ruled, from their present unsustainable predicament.[2] The Trustees and Advisors of the CRCE are bound by its constitution to disassociate themselves from the arguments and conclusions of authors. Our hope remains that this study by a group of independent economists in Poland, with comments by Professor Brzeski and Jan Rostowski, will throw new light on the present soul-searching in Poland and other countries of Eastern Europe.

Ljubo Sirc

---

1. Cf. *The Economist* of November 28, 1987, accepts this view and writes at the end of the first leader on p.16:
   If the Russians and East Europeans did the sort of dash for freedom from controls into which Ludwig Erhard led West Germany in 1948, they might have a post-1948

1

West German sort of economic miracle. If they do a half-dash, they will have Yugoslavia's post-1948 sort of economic mess. Mr Gorbachev dare not risk a full dash because most of his Politburo are like junta members who would not tolerate the IMF. But he would gain if one communist country introduced reforms that could succeed, preferably the one that wants to. He should telephone Budapest, and say "imitate Erhard".

2. May we draw attention to another contribution to the same debate – *NSZZ 'Solidarnosc' on Reforming the Polish Economy.* (Approved by Lech Walesa) published by the co-ordinating office of 'Solidarnosc', 9 avenue de la Joyeuse Entrée, 1040 Brussels, Belgium, 1987.

Preface

Andrzej Brzeski

This Report, by unnamed Warsaw economists, was apparently written in two stages. The first part of *Poland: Stagnation, Collapse or Growth* was completed over two years ago; the second, a year later. Despite the delay in its publication, the text, though no longer current in every detail, has lost none of its fundamental topicality. Just as the title suggests, the future of Poland's economy remains in question: continuing stagnation, even collapse, present a distinct possibility. Indeed, if anything, things seem to have gotten worse with time. And the means to recovery have become even more problematic than before. The difficulties and doubts surrounding the much talked about "Second Stage of the Reform" – its implementation has already begun – loom larger than ever. Thus, the publication by the Centre for Research into Communist Economies of this highly critical assessment of the Polish economy is timely, especially since the text is not available elsewhere.

The report makes for instructive reading. The reader is disabused by any notion that state ownership and central planning are likely to bestow economic benefits. At one time, communist regimentation and inefficiencies may have been considered a trade-off, though not necessarily worthwhile, for accelerated growth. "They eye our efficiency, we eye their growth," was the way Peter Wiles put it. Other alleged advantages were said to include: price stability and more equal distribution, as well as wide accessibility of health and educational services, and, last but no least, effective checks on negative externalities. The authors put such ideas to rest. Forty years of communism in Poland have obviously produced altogether different results. What emerges is a picture of near-chaos: an input-input economy, with arbitrary prices distorting all calculations and inhibiting rational conduct, domestically and abroad. The classic critique of collectivist planning (by Mises, Hayek *et al.*), could be amply illustrated by examples taken from this eyewitness account. In addition, inflation is on the rise, approaching Latin American rates: social services, in particular, health, steadily deteriorate, while, due to industrial pollution, an ecological catastrophe seems to be in the making. Altogether this is an instance of colossal and multifaceted mismanagement. Only the peasant agriculture, because it has succeeded in

3

resisting collectivization pressures in the past, provides a modicum of relief.

For a variety of reasons, Poland is the most dramatic and best publicized of communist troubles with the economy. Yet is is hardly unique. The reader, familiar with other "basket cases" of the communist world, may well ponder the more fundamental implications. For his study of *Economic Reforms in Polish Industry* (1973), the late Janusz G. Zielinski used as a motto a passage from a historian's work: "It has been the fate of Poland, more than of most countries, that outsiders have been mainly concerned to see in it a spectacular object lesson, hurrying on from interest in the Poles themselves to find evidence for general truths of wider application." And why not? The Polish economic system, deserving of close scrutiny as it may be, is but a specimen of a *genus* that can afflict many. A report from and about Poland gives universal warning against the pitfalls of marxist-leninist social engineering.

The unnamed authors also show how very complex and frustrating is the task of would be reformers of communism. We are reminded that in Poland "there have been (too) many programs for overcoming the crisis and speeding up the economy." All of them, evidently, to no avail: *plus ça change, plus c'est la même chose.* Why should things turn out differently next time around, one is bound to ask. Even in the present era, this is a valid question which goes beyond the issue of skepticism borne of pervious experience – that of years 1957, 1965 and 1982, to mention only the crucial dates in the history of Polish attempts at economic reform. It also is a question which clearly transcends pure economics.

The authors sketch out some reform proposals of their own: free market pricing, competition, currency convertibility, fiscal discipline, monetary restraint, all sensible measures, although short of the logical conclusion of privatization or quasi-privatization as the ultimate solution. But these recommendations are offered, as it were, hypothetically, in disregard of the immediate realities of time and place. The part of the text dealing with the proposals bears the telling title "An Abstract Scenario for a Transition to a New System." The adjective "abstract" is the key; it emphasizes the lack of conditions for cleaning up the existing economic mess at this juncture. Even so, the authors insist, there is a glimmer of hope. The manifest failure of the present system engenders a "readiness to abandon it and to adopt a different system, a different economy ... such attitudes are noticeable even among ... party and government circle."

In the already mentioned book on economic reforms, Zielinski, who was their ardent advocate, rightly noted: "The most important conditions for the successful implementation of comprehensive economic reforms are, probably, political in nature.' By this, he meant at the time of writing, some fifteen years ago, that a ruling (communist) party must be united and strong to take on the risks of revamping the economy. What he overlooked however, and what is suggested now, is the likelihood of more fundamental reforms – along the lines of the report and beyond – out of the communists' weakness *vis-à-vis* the society. This kind of partial self-liquidation of the marxist-leninist "vanguard of the proletariat" may be in store for Poland, according to the view expressed in the report. If so, the weakening of the party during the "Solidarity" period must have set the stage, as did the erosion of party prerogatives under the military regime.

These, it must be said, are speculations rather than prognostications; there are far too many unknowns in the historic process which will decide the future of Poland's economic system. Its evolution will, in all probability, continue to be interwoven with broader developments, above all with the still highly uncertain Soviet *perestroika* and *glasnost*.

For the shorter run, there is the unfolding of the "Second Stage of the Reform": a pseudo-referendum, the inevitable reduction of living standards etc. No one really knows how well this will work either. Admittedly, the official blueprint is not without merit. Its adoption, by relaxing the grip of the central plan and making prices more realistic, *could* conceivably bring positive results. A recent World Bank preview of the reform proposals was outright optimistic, speaking of a promise of "faster growth, greater competitiveness ... faster technological progress, a more rapid improvement in living standards and a smaller external debt." This may be so. For the sake of the long suffering Polish people, one would like to believe it.

Nonetheless, whether a *sine qua non* degree of social stability can be maintained throughout an even lilmited overhaul of the Polish economy is not at all clear. The immediate cost is sure to be heavy, while the rewards are conjectural and in the future. The situation smacks of a paradox: having forcibly inflected their system upon an unwilling nation, the Polish communists are perhaps ready to roll it back a bit. But they do not quite know how, and, besides, may well be prevented from trying, by ... the working class.

Recently, a journalist's account (Tad Szulc in *Los Angeles Times,* November 18) raised an alarm: "An unholy alliance between Solidarity and hard-line communists ... could conceivably undermine the Polish government ... the Polish Reform movement, formally launched last month ... is being fought by the democratic opposition." The warning, no doubt meant to be helpful to General Jaruzelski's reform efforts, entirely misses the point. It is not the opposition's meddling that threatens to derail economic reforms. On the contrary, bent on preserving their monopoly of power, the communists themselves, imperil the reform, by their inability to enlist the support of authentic social forces, including, needless to say, Solidarity. Given the extent of the damage to be undone, and the dismal circumstances, the task is staggering. It will prove difficult to accomplish even with Solidarity's full cooperation; without such a support, it is well nigh impossible. This publication makes one appreciate why it is so.

November 21, 1987

☆ *Andrzej Brzeski is Professor of Economics at the University of California, Davis.*

Poland:
Stagnation, Collapse or Growth?

Translated from Polish by
Barteusz

Introduction

A look at the Polish economy on the threshold of the second half of 1985 must provide a considerable stock of information about production, exchange and consumption and should offer a photograph of the economy at the moment, though the moment can of course be defined as a month, a quarter or even a half-year. At the same time information concerning the past and a knowledge of economic principles should enable us to predict the tendencies and trends in economic processes and thus project the probable future course of the economy.

Therefore it has to be an understanding look, interpreting the meaning of perceived facts, phenomena and information and their interrelationship in a broader systemic context. It will be an objective look as far as facts are concerned and fair in regard to assessment. But the criteria and standards by which we shall judge will not be neutral, but entirely partial — partial, of course, to what is right.

One more point requires explanation. Our knowledge of facts about the state of the Polish economy is drawn both from personal experiences (our own and other people's) and statistical data. Are these data reliable? Is the official information on the economy given (and censored) by the authorities true? Official Polish statistics do not provide a true and complete picture of the economy, but the deviation from truth consists mainly in the omission of certain phenomena. Another form of statistical lie is false classification and division, which blur certain phenomena. Finally, statistical distortion occurs due to the difficulties in measurement of value, which result from the existing system of prices. However, it is only rarely that false figures are given, and if they are, they are relatively easy to detect. Statistical information should not be left out, but it must be read properly, interpreted, and supplemented.

The picture of the economy which emerges from the present study signals the approach of a new crisis at a time when the previous crisis of the early 1980's has not yet ended. Although it was officially announced from the highest rostrum at the end of 1984 that the crisis had been overcome, this was clearly wishful thinking. During 1984 the Polish economy was still operating considerably below its 1978 level; GNP was 15%

down, and per capita income 20% down from the peak year of the 1970s. And this with capital assets 25% greater. Thus we are still stuck in the morass – the rate of growth of production decreases, new disproportions appear, equilibrium is further disturbed and tensions increase. A new stage in the fatal recurrence of political and economic crises which have marked the economic history of the Polish People's Republic for the last forty years is now beginning. We can distinguish three such cycles, in which economic collapse (in the years 1955-56, 1969-70 and 1980-82) brought severe disruption, political upheaval and a change in leadership. If the phenomena we try to investigate in the present study persist and intensify, a fourth crisis will follow.

The method we have adopted consists in statistical analysis supplemented with information from other selected sources from the key branches of the economy, those that determine the fundamental economic parameters and are the first to signal changes in trends. These are industrial production, the progress and fluctuations of which are quite accurately measured by the GUS index, energy production, the labour market, which is showing increasing strain, and the level of incomes together with its influence on market equilibrium. In these areas, phenomena occur which allow an up-to-date assessment of the state of the economy. These current processes go on against a background of other sectors where the rhythm of change is slower and whose influence on the whole is less spectacular, but longer lasting: agriculture, investment and foreign trade. In our analyses of individual economic sectors we do not confine ourselves to recording phenomena, but endeavour to link them with certain general tendencies, and explain them by referring to certain theoretical arguments based on the principles of economics.

In the second part of the study we present an analysis of fundamental features of the preliminary plan for the years 1986-90, and on this basis we sketch a scenario of events which, should it come true, would ultimately lead to a fourth upheaval in the structure of government in Poland. The social, political and economic consequences of such a course of events would be even greater than in the previous cycles. Of course we may be wrong about the timing of the scenario. Certain processes may be postponed or delayed. But the direction of the process sketched in the scenario is calculated with a high degree of certainty. The question is not 'if' but 'when'?

The authors of the present study wish not to confine themselves to the role of observers, but to formulate and put forward an aim and a programme under which social forces could be mobilized to act to break the morbid sequence of crises. This aim and programme consist in attacking what we call the 'idle' sector of our economy until it is eliminated. The identification of the idle sector as the chief cause – beside the wasteful system of functioning of the economy – of our progressive economic decline and poverty is one of the aims of the present study.

Part I

THE STATE OF THE ECONOMY IN 1985

1. Production in the First Half of 1985 – A New Crisis

We will begin with the simplest but most recent matters: Polish industrial production was losing what little momentum it had even in 1984, and in certain branches was actually decreasing. This was not happening in the severe winter months but in the second quarter, in beautiful spring and summer sunshine. Figures given in a GUS* announcement leave no room to doubt this. During the first five months of 1985 Polish statisticians recorded a mere 1.6% growth in the total industrial output (compared with the same period of 1984) which, given the low accuracy of the survey, must be simply described as minimal growth. Worse, however, is the pattern for particular months. In March industry seemed to stir after the winter months and a 4.5% increase was observed, but by April the winter weariness returned and the increase amounted to only 3.6%. May, with an increase of 2.1%, proved still more sluggish. These data cast doubts on the main figure of the GUS announcement covering the first half-year, claiming a 2% increase in industrial production. We generally assume that GUS data are statistically reliable; this figure however, has to be considered spurious. This conclusion can be arrived at from the following calculation: with a 1.6% rise in output during the first five months, the 2% increase in the production for the half-year would be possible only if June output increased by as much as 4% in the so-called real time. And since June 1985 had one more Sunday than June 1984, in a comparable time, output in June 1985 would need to be more than 8% greater than in June 1984. This would be an extraordinary success, which the GUS report would not fail to highlight, whereas the announcement, contrary to the accepted practice, was discreetly silent about the fulfilment of industrial targets in June. If we assume that, at best, the increase in production in June was the same as in May, the growth in the six months could not have exceeded 1.7% compared with a planned increase of 4%. The actual growth was probably still lower and GUS is likely to correct it in due course, as it has more than once before, explaining that the figures in the half-year announcements were only estimates. The current explanation of this unexpected leap in the half-year figure was that the initial May figure was too low. The GUS announcement for the first five months stated that production in May 1985 was 2.1% higher than in May 1984. After a month, when it turned out that the six months period would look dismal, GUS counted again and found some reserves: the May 1985 increase jumped to 5.0% and saved the half-year. It is a manoeuvre done on paper, temporarily possible with aggregate figures such as 'industrial production'. In the months to come a further correction will doubtless be made.

The first half-year in industry therefore closed with the lowest growth for three years, and 1985 as a whole may turn out simply disastrous, with a negative increase in GNP! That would mean that the country was entering a new phase of crisis.

* Editor's note: Central Statistical Office.

Some figures specifically indicate that such a course of events is by no means impossible. Compared with the same period last year, production for five months decreased by 4% in the metal industry, by 3% in the chemical industry, by 1% in electric power generating (coal!) and by as much as 9% in mining. Production of tractors, cars, washing machines, steel, paper and footwear were lower than the previous year – the decreases ranging from 1% to 5%. But the production of nitrogen fertilisers dropped by as much as 22%, and of cement by 17%, to a level below any other year of the crisis. Obviously, a decrease in the production of an important commodity by 20% or even by 10% must disrupt all users of this commodity to some extent. And this is what happened. Suddenly, there was again no cement in Poland. As recently as 1984 cement was on unrestricted sale and purchases were encouraged; and in mid-1985 there was none because there was a gap of 25% in relation to the plans (and material balance). Obviously, this 25% covers all marginal buyers who are not eligible for priority, e.g. individual construction of homes. But a gap of this size spreads into further areas in a chain-reaction; gaps appear in other, less closely related branches and the economy takes a plunge. The effects of the lack of cement can be perceived in the construction industry (weaker growth in May), and still more clearly in investment: by the end of April less than 7% of the year's plan was completed, and in housing less than 4%! In the first half of the year, 12% fewer flats were completed than in 1984.

What had happened then? How did this sudden collapse in industry (following a relatively good year 1984) come about? Why this recession in the third year of the so-called three-year plan which was supposed to end the period of 'recovering from the crisis' and restore the economy's capacity for balanced development? Is it the dreaded technological crisis coming? This does not seem to be the case yet, but the worst is still ahead. The root causes of the sudden industrial weakening fit into the general model of the 'contracting reproduction' of a socialist economy. In the course of 1983-84 the economy used all its easily tapped reserves, which permitted a rise of production from the lowest level of 1982. But now, further growth can be sustained only by drawing on deeper reserves, and this involves the use of intensive methods. Meanwhile, the available production factors are still fully utilised and a large portion of the products thus obtained is directed to idle or useless applications. And so we have enormous waste, both of inputs and of output. It is as though someone strenuously drew water from an ever deeper well and immediately poured some of the water (hardly a negligible amount) onto dry sand, so that not enough remained to quench his thirst. Obviously, this operation can be sustained only as long as the supply of extensive production factors is not exhausted. A system usually starts to collapse at its weakest point, as a chain breaks at its weakest link. In Poland in 1985 two factors proved to be the weakest links: coal and the labour force.

2. The Problem of Coal – The Limits

The decisive and growing importance of coal in the Polish economy has long been recognised. In the period of decreased coal production (in 1981 it fell to 163m. tons) government programmes for economic recovery loudly proclaimed that once the 40m. tons shortfall in coal output was made up the difficulties would be overcome. 'Give us coal,' miners were urged, 'and we will give the country economic stability.' Today coal mining has regained its previous rate of output and exports are also near pre-crisis level. But now more coal is needed; the economy's consumption has grown. The mining industry cannot provide more coal, however; the maximum is 193-195m. tons a year. And even this level is only achieved by wasteful exploitation: the deposits are not mined rationally and 50% or more of the coal is left underground beyond retrieval; lost for ever. Mining is carried out under cities, and the emptied galleries are not properly filled with sand and water, so that damage to buildings as a result of subsidence is increasing sharply. Finally, in marginal mines costs exceed the industry average five or perhaps tenfold; closing down these mines would radically reduce the costs of production and lower the output level to rational dimensions: 150-160m. tons. This, however, given the economy's energy consumption rates, is not enough.

When four months after the end of winter, energy was still in short supply, extraordinary measures were adopted. In early July 1985 an extraordinary inter-departmental conference on coal was held in Katowice. It revised the fuel and energy balance yet again and discussed the difficulties in transporting coal, but, most important, it introduced limits on fuel and energy for industry. Energy limits for industrial buyers are a novelty, and mean that in the second half of the year, and especially in the autumn-winter peak, industry will have little chance of making up for the production delays of the first half-year. Meanwhile, the economy's energy consumption is growing. In the first half of 1985, with an industrial production increase (according to GUS) of 2%, the consumption of electrical energy in industry rose by 2.5%.

The imposition of energy limits on companies indicates that when faced with a severe shortage of an important production factor the authorities forget about all the reform and revert to central allocation, the method familiar and tested (and found wanting). This is very inauspicious. The basic task facing the Polish economy is to improve efficiency, including the efficiency of energy use. When demand for a commodity is greater than supply, its use has to be selective. The problem is the mechanism of selection. The economic reform stipulates that central allocation of capital goods should be limited, and raw materials increasingly bought by companies at equilibrium prices in free transactions. The difference lies in the fact that somebody else will get the scarce material as a result of decentralised purchase. But it will not be a random somebody; the material will be obtained by the user who will produce the greater economic effect. The user who gets the material (coal) at an equilibrium price will use it to manufacture an end-product whose price will cover the cost of the coal; and if the price of the end product is an equilibrium price, the purchaser will buy only as much as he needs, and this use of coal will have been socially justified. Manufacturers with high energy consumption will lose in competition with other purchasers, and will not be able to afford coal for inefficient use.

In comparison with this mechanism, central allocation is crude: the material is given to the buyer who will use it the way the central allocating authority deems most appropriate; he gets as much as he is able to bargain for – and he always demands more than he actually needs as he has no incentive to use it economically – and he gets it regardless of whether he is efficient or wasteful.

The reason for maintaining and indeed extending central allocation is of course the first point: the authorities prefer to decide to whom to give, whom to ignore. But other conditions which are indispensable for the abandoning of central allocation are also not fulfilled. The price of coal is not an equilibrium price since, despite a dramatic (fourfold) rise in 1982, it is still kept far below the (growing) costs of production, although the economists involved in introducing the reform point to the necessity of increasing it further. But a government document in April 1985 dealing with financial policy for the next five years stated that 'it is not anticipated that the selling price of coal will rise to the level ensuring full profitability of coal production before the end of the 1980s *because of the heavy influence of coal on the prices of other products.*' Actually, the reasoning should be the reverse: precisely because of the fact that coal is lthe energy input into the production of thousands of goods, its price should be raised to the equilibrium level since this is the only way for the prices of those 'coal-based' goods to reach a proper level. It should be added that for correct economic calculation coal prices should be raised not only to the level of profitability, but to the level of prices obtained for exports (the dollar price multiplied by the marginal rate of exchange, now about 200 zlotys to the dollar). The mines would then not only cover their own production costs, together with the so-called profit overheads, but would yield a profit which had a full economic justification. At the same time, the higher price of coal would induce all users to economise on it, as it would then be worthwhile to bear other costs to save expensive coal. All these economic subtleties, however, are beyond the planners in Poland, and the price of coal will remain unchanged. But since there will not be enough coal to satisfy the economy's present consumption, the economic distribution mechanism will continue to be suppressed in favour of administrative allocation. A country which is the fourth coal producer in the world, and second (!) in per capita production, is going to have widespread rationing of coal: in industry, in transport, in utilities. When someone raised the question of individual buyers during the Katowice conference (hundreds of thousands of houses are heated by coal in Poland), the response was that the supply might improve only if it was possible to save coal in industry. That means never, for it is well known that no recipient of allocation will ever use less than he is allotted because next time he would get a smaller allocation.

3. The Labour Market – Manpower Shortage

Many other goods, as well as coal, are in short supply in Poland, but the root of most of these shortages is the shortage of manpower. From the economic point of view, this problem is much more difficult than that with coal, but it is equally paradoxical. The country which has had (for decades) the highest birth rate in Europe, which boasts one of the highest participation rates (about 51%), which still has enormous reserves of labour in agriculture (25% of all employed), experiences a shortage of labour. In other countries, there is unemployment, and hundreds of candidates for one post, whereas in Poland there are no applicants for jobs either simple or sophisticated. Everybody who can (and wants to) work is already employed, but there is an enormous unsatisfied demand for labour, from state-owned companies, factories and institutions, and from the population. Both sources have a great deal of money which creates an immense demand for all goods and services, and thus for labour to provide these goods and services. In this respect the Polish economy is flourishing, experiencing a boom and even – using the language of textbooks – 'overheating', though the overheating has been present for decades. But this only means that certain textbook terms and economic categories are not appropriate for description and especially assessment of an economy like that of Poland, and additional conceptual tools have to be used to explain this singular phenomenon. We will try to do this, but first let us dwell a little longer on the labour market. New employees are wanted first of all by state-owned companies, big factories, municipal utility enterprises, trade agencies, construction companies – they all clamour for more workers. Every day, newspapers publish whole columns of advertisements by state-owned companies declaring that they will 'employ immediately' what is usually as full a list of specialisations as can be imagined: from accountants, turners, millers, to diggers, errand boys, cleaners and shop assistants. They need everybody, and have to compete against the growing private sector (individual agriculture, private industry, or simply households that are turned into mini-workshops), which offers better pay than the so-called nationalised sector, and will allow no unused surplus of labour.

This state of affairs creates an enormous imbalance on the labour market of the opposite kind to that in capitalist countries. In relation to the extensive demand, the supply of labour is too small. There is a lack of manpower in factories which, equipped with expensive machines and fixed assets, work only one shift (and are fortunate if it is a full one). There is a lack of manpower in services, trade and utilities. Tens, hundreds of shops in cities have their opening hours curtailed or are closed altogether due to the lack of staff; in post-offices, railway stations and savings banks every second counter is unmanned for lack of staff. In big cities especially, where the situation is worst, it is very difficult to get anything done if it is connected with a service rendered by a state enterprise. It is even difficult to buy a newspaper or cigarettes because only one in three kiosks is open.

Newspapers daily publish whole columns of classified advertisements and we can choose between any number of firms to insulate our windows and doors, repair household appliances immediately, decorate our homes, and provide numerous other services. What is happening? People are abandoning their jobs in state-owned factories, steel plants, mines, construction companies, offices and institutions and getting new jobs in private firms or private agriculture, where farmer-workers are becoming farmers. Recently the press was glad to report that in the Lenin Steel Plant the egress of employees which had been decimating the staff of the biggest factory in Poland had been finally stopped. But mines have fared much worse; the Minister of Mining stated that five thousand people left in June 1985 alone, for instance.

In this way the spontaneous flow of labour is doing what neither central planners nor the so-called economic reform has achieved: restructuring the economy. Of course, it is on a small scale, but it is already significant. Official statistics state that almost a million people are employed in the so-called non-nationalised economy, excluding agriculture, i.e. nearly 10% of all non-agricultural labour, and since nobody plans or subsidises them, we can be sure that if they can earn their living, it means that their work is useful, and their production needed by the country.

This is not so in the predominant part of the nationalised sector. This sector can be divided into two parts: that which serves the people, and the other which works for the needs of the system and has nothing to do with needs of the population. From the population's point of view, the latter is an idle sector. This name, which, more than 250 years ago, was used by Quesnay to describe the social-economic structure of pre-revolutionary France, today fits a large part of the production apparatus in the Polish People's Republic and the social structure it serves. It is this huge idle sector that causes the permanent imbalance on both the so-called labour market and on all other markets or quasi-markets. It is also the reason why the signs of economic boom, in the shape of constant, intense, and even aggressive demand which would elsewhere be an indication of prosperity, in Poland accompany a dramatic crisis leading towards an economic breakdown.

The mechanism which generates the demand for labour (and other production factors) from the idle sector, and from the whole of the 'nationalised' economy, operates as follows: enterprises have to meet their production goals which, despite the supposed abolition of 'plan directives', are given to them by their 'founding organs' (ministries) or by other means (operating programmes, government orders) in such a way that they constitute the basis of their evaluation by the government. These tasks (plans, programmes, orders) have to be completed. Faced with a lack of raw materials and the unreliability of ageing machines, the surest and most flexible reserve of capacity is labour, which can always be used to compensate for the shortcomings of other production factors. Thus employment should be maximised, or at least maintained at its present level. Labour costs in Poland are very low and do not exceed 15% of total production value, and in any case increased costs can always be included in the price of products calculated by the so-called cost method, i.e. total costs plus profit overheads. An additional impulse to this policy is the fact that such relative abundance of labour in a firm does not force an increase in work efficiency, thus allowing slack organisation and discipline, which are of course comfortable for both managment and staff.

Consequently, the whole nationalised sector aims to retain all the labour already employed and to take on more if it can be obtained from the labour market. Any improvement in labour utilisation, any redundancies or release are out of the question. As far as employment is concerned, the economic reform was defeated from the start. For the expectation that making companies independent, combined with strengthened economic incentives, would produce a huge surplus of labour and might even trigger unemployment proved totally wrong. In order to prevent the expected unemployment, several hundred thousand people were allowed to retire prematurely in 1981. Meanwhile, the economic reform has changed nothing and nationalised companies continue to call for more people.

Excessive employment in that part of the nationalised economy which serves the population is only half of the problem. Light industry, the food industry, retail trade, numerous branches manufacturing consumer goods, construction, and finally the whole 'non-productive' sphere – education, culture, health service – and utilities all lack labour. These industries frequently work only one shift, but even if they make inefficient use of the labour they are still socially useful, providing the economy with products and services which create the population's means of subsistence. This is not true of the idle sector. The main part of heavy industry, most of mining, nearly all the engineering industry, including an enormous military complex, and finally most contractors working on construction, notably on big investment projects continued from the Gierek period, all these constitute the main reservoir of frozen labour and an enormous pump sucking labour from the labour market. But unlike those in the productive sector, people working in the idle sector do not produce either for themselves or for the rest of society. Their production, which consumes materials, machines and their own labour however, is a leak which is never fed back into the economy, does not reproduce the capital invested, including the expenditure on labour. With such an extensive and inefficient use of labour in the entire state sector – and no return at all in the case of the idle sector – labour reproduction is contracting. In spite of the fact that biological reproduction of labour in Poland is still broad, social reproduction of this factor in the state economy is decreasing. In individual branches or so-called non-productive spheres, not only are there no people to increase output or broaden the range of services, but there are even too few to maintain the present level. A temporary rise in the egress, some local disturbance on the labour market, is enough to decimate the work force in factories; machines are left unmanned, other jobs undone, and output falls.

Of course, the economic authorities are trying to prevent the growing shortages. But the simplest solution – intensifying labour management – is out of the question. Although all the recommendations and expectations connected with the much trumpeted economic reform envisage such action, in practice there has been no change in the way the economy functions; there is neither pressure nor incentive to intensify the use of production factors, especially labour.

Instead of improving employment efficiency, labour allocation has been adopted. Since 1983 employment offices have been assigning prospective employees to specific companies. But employment allocation proves to be much more difficult than the rationing of coal or meat and cannot be carried out without harsh regulations and a vast bureaucratic apparatus; allocation cannot create plenty from an acute deficit. Thus, despite regulations enforcing priorities (e.g. the ban on directing employment seekers to private business), the efforts of the employment offices to direct labour have not helped at all.

4. Pressure on Wages – Effective Indexation

The permanent shortage of labour not only has a crucial impact on production, but also constitutes an important influence on living conditions. Ease of finding a job, the ability to choose among a variety of jobs, and competition between employers give an average person a certain social comfort, which leads, on the one hand to slack work discipline and, on the other, to demands for pay rises. Of course, the costs of this comfort, in the form of a malfunctioning economy, impose a burden on the employee too, in his role as buyer, consumer, passenger, or petitioner. Despite this, people appreciate this state of affairs and use it, on the one hand, to slow down their pace of work (a very high percentage of working hours is wasted). Throughout the 1980s in Poland there has been steady, occasionally even rising, pressure on wages, resulting in an annual average rate of nominal pay increases of over 20%. Some pay rises are granted at the central level, and so apply all over the country, but the main locus is individual work establishments. Partly independent companies yield to those pressures and can even go as far as to initiate pay increases in order to stop the egress of employees to better paid jobs in the private sector. Here, too, the economic reform was deficient: it did not determine when pay was to be increased (only an increase in efficiency was supposed to be rewarded), nor did it create economic pressure to curb pay rises to what a company could afford. It appears that here, too, capitalist resistance to pay rises cannot be imitated simply because there are no entrepreneurs who would be struggling for their own economic survival in such a confrontation. Managers of state-owned factories are only officials who do not feel personally threatened by pay demands and have appeared extremely soft, or even taken the workers' side against the decision of the central plan. They have turned against the only weapon the central planners still wield against wage pressure – the special tax called PFAZ (National Professional Activation Fund, or something like a tax to fund anticipated unemployment). This tax is paid by a company from its profits when its pay increases exceed its output increase index. The burden is painful for a company because it deprives it of resources needed for its development. Therefore, the tax has been the subject of much protest from companies, culminating in the first quarter of 1985. When it appeared that owing to harsh weather conditions output could not be raised to a level which would allow wage rises without incurring PFAZ tax while the work force pressed more and more strongly for increases (anticipating the announced food price increases), managers of companies mutinied against the chief tax collector, the finance minister, and refused to pay the PFAZ. The minister gave in and agreed to suspend PFAZ payments due for the first quarter, ostensibly in order to let companies make up for delays in production (which was to be paid for at an appropriately higher rate). But output in the second quarter failed to improve, the delays were not made up and the PFAZ again became a bone of contention. Meanwhile, the suspension of the tax created a revenue gap of more than ten billion zlotys.

The growing pressure on wages, originating in big companies, meant that the incomes of other segments of the population had to be increased, although this was done with reluctance in the so-called non-productive sphere; nominal incomes of farmers were also growing and, finally, pensions were raised though they still lagged behind. All in all, the population's nominal income grew by over 26% in the first six months of 1985 (accompanied, let us remember, by an increase in output of only 2%). The average monthly pay in the middle of 1985 was 20,000 zlotys, i.e. 20% more than at the same time in 1984, but for some trades rates exceeded this average severalfold: in May 1985 a bricklayer at a private construction job charged 5,000 zlotys a day!

The expanding incomes were not matched by corresponding growth in the supply of goods and services on the market. There was more or less equilibrium on the food market (even for meat sold off the ration), although it was accomplished at the price of severe impoverishment of variety; the supply of goods turned out by private businesses was rising, too. But the basic market in industrial products remained undersupplied and characterised by the same striking shortages of entire ranges of products that have been haunting the economy since the late 1970s. The position was somewhat better with footwear; there was even a significant improvement in supply of rubber boots (important for farmers and young people). But with clothing things were still in a bad way; there was no underwear at all! (Cotton is not imported in sufficient quantity and the production of artificial fibres is falling). It was very bad with most furniture, still worse with household appliances, sports goods, stationery, and books, light bulbs and sanitary, plumbing, and construction materials. Given this scarcity, bribery, profiteering, and black markets flourish.

If the population's growing income does not induce an adequate increase in market supply (because production either is not growing or is not channelled to the market), it must induce an increase in prices. But if even this is not sufficient to compensate for income growth, then queues lengthen and money is deposited in forced savings. And this is precisely what has happened. According to GUS the cost of living rose by almost 13% in the first six months of 1985; since market supply, calculated in fixed prices, grew by 2% during the same period, the value of the supply side on the market increased by 15.2% (113.0 x 102.0 = 115.2, while the demand side rose by 26.3%. This excess could not be spent. And indeed, the population's expenditure grew by only 15.6%, almost exactly the same rate as the value of goods and services supplied. The remaining 55% of the increment in incomes was accumulated in financial resources which in the first half of 1985 were almost 4.5 times what they had been a year before, forming a new, additional inflationary overhang of almost 350 billion zlotys.

This fact undermines the official claim of growing real wages. Juxtaposition of nominal wage growth and the increase in the cost of living leads to the conclusion that real wages did increase, and by over 5% (118.6: 112.8 = 105.1). This disagrees with the prevailing feeling among the people and it is that feeling that is correct. For if we subtract from the nominal wage growth (18.6) the unspent 55%, we will see that the nominal increase to which there was a corresponding supply of goods amounted only to 8.4% (108.4: 112.8 = 0.96). It is little wonder, then, that commercial stocks grew. Luckily for the authorities, people are nominalists and treat the additional inflationary overhang deposited in a bank or kept in cash as an increase of actual value.

The conclusion is that although the authorities managed to keep the increase in prices to around 14%, they did not manage to hold incomes within the same limits. In these circumstances, the restriction of prices is an administrative operation and not an economic one and resulted in a new inflationary overhang intensifying and disequilibrium on the market.

Despite that, the statistical increase of real wages (and other forms of incomes translated into income per recipient) by 5% is a fact of profound importance. It does not satisfy the people, but it constitutes an additional burden for the economy and creates problems for the authorities. It was a forced increase which the 1985 Central Annual Plan did not provide for, as it assumed there would be no increase in wages. Why did events get out of hand in this way?

We said above that the pressure on wages results from the state of the labour market, from an enormous shortage of labour! But these 'market laws' could become apparent only when people selling their labour on the market were sufficiently sovereign in their decisions. It is only then that the major employer, the state, has to pay a higher price for their work, that is, bribe them with higher wages. And here lies a political problem. Working people in Poland, and especially workers in big companies, won social sovereignty five years ago creating *Solidarity*. And despite the fact that after sixteen months *Solidarity* was banned and its official structures crushed, the sovereignty of workers has been maintained and thanks to that they can effectively stand up for their rights any time their basic interests are violated. The spokesman for these interests and potential organiser of struggle when they are endangered is the residual underground structure of *Solidarity*. Our analysis of the economic situation shows how great the importance of the democratic opposition is, above all of those union structures that exist in companies or that can reach the workforce, and how great a role was played by the Provisional Coordinating Commission (TKK),* too, when it assessed the situation country-wide and drew up the position working people should adopt toward particular events and government policies.

The authorities know about this threat full well and act to prevent it, pouring out a stream of paper money which raises nominal wages and calms tempers down for a few months, as people are temporarily placated with a nominal rise. It is only later that they confront and reflect upon prices and difficulties in availability.

This is how the meat price rise on 1st July 1985 should be understood. The employees of big companies had received more than compensation for it during the first four months of the year in the form of bonuses, profit-sharing, and other such titles invented to pay the people to keep quiet. And on 1st July, when the price of (rationed) meat went up by 15%, which increased the cost of living by 2%, keep quiet they did. But this does not mean that *Solidarity's* action was a failure, or the TKK appeal for a protest strike was immaterial. It was useful, even though not fully carried out. The appeal was a threat to strike repeated for months and needed to render the strike itself unnecessary. If, however, the authorities interpret the fact that 1st July passed peacefully to mean that *Solidarity* is no longer able to organise resistance and they undertake some larger price action, they may well be making a big mistake.

* Editor's note: The highest underground body of *Solidarity*.

This whole wage pressure mechanism, which has now extended to other forms of income too, means that in Poland there is effectively a system of income indexation. Wages (and other incomes) keep climbing abreast of prices, and occasionally even overtake them. It is of course not happening in an orderly way; it is an elemental process which takes place in a concrete struggle between social-political forces.

5. Inflation – Here to Stay

Starting a mechanism of elemental wage and income indexation obviously constitutes a driving force of inflation. It is not the only or even the main cause of inflation. Yet the inflationary factor emerging from the demand side is spectacular: wages chasing prices, prices in turn chasing wages. Still, it must be borne in mind that, apart from the price-wage spiral on the demand side, there are two other, and stronger, factors operating in the Polish economy generating inflation. They are cost and supply. Costs of production rise independently of wages in Poland, mainly because of waste in the form of excessive wear, inferior quality of products, etc. This growth of costs is transferred either directly to prices, or, in the form of subsidies, to the budget, which is ultimately covered by prices too. The supply factor stimulates inflation by limiting market supply or causing structural discrepancies between supply and demand and encouraging a rise in prices to restore equilibrium (at a reduced supply). Both these sources of inflation may be regarded as primary, while the pay factor is secondary (if not caused mainly by a shortage of labour), for it is a response to the movement of prices caused by the other two factors. The authorities' drive to freeze wages aims at shifting onto the people the results of the supply inflationary factor which is caused by the anti-market economic policy and by the cost inflationary factor which is a consequence of the system's inefficiency. Wages and other incomes of the population have been serving a shock-absorbing function for the costs of policies and of the system for decades, which permitted inflation to be kept low. But since *Solidarity* the absorber has grown stiffer and the inflationary spiral has been gaining momentum.

Inflation in Poland is not yet at a gallop and it is far from the hyperinflation of Latin America. Some 20-25% a year is a rate one can still live with. But the distinctive socialist peculiarity of this inflation, that makes it harder to live with, is that a large number of the prices concerned are not equilibrium prices. Thus many goods cannot be bought for the prices used in calculating inflation. Socialist inflation, therefore, consists of two segments: that expressed by the movement of prices, and what we might call 'queue inflation', or diminishing availability of products. These segments are mutually off-setting – when price inflation grows, queue inflation is somewhat reduced; when queue inflation increases, price inflation must have slackened. In order fully to 'monetarise' Polish inflation, theoretically a single price leap of 20-100% (about 70% on average) would have to be made, after which a quicker rate of price rises would have to be permitted to maintain equilibrium prices at all times. Current writing on the economy in Poland keeps urging the government to aim at equilibrium prices. This is in keeping with the recommendations of the economic reform, constitutes a precondition of a normal market, and bestows full economic significance on money. In practice, however, maintaining equilibrium on the market at any price level is impossible in this system, and the people do not dream of this either. People are nominalists both in pay and in price and prefer the fiction of low price, for which they can buy the product only with much effort or by chance, to the certainty and convenience of a high price purchase.

In this way, the twofold inflation is maintained, adding to the existing chaos in the economy. One way it does this is to aggravate the deviations and irrationalities of the price structure. There are three types of prices in Poland: official, regulated, and contracted or free. The reform provided for the area of free, or equilibrium prices to expand. In practice, the trend is in the opposite direction: the reform being limited and unsuccessful, more and more official and regulated prices exacerbate queue inflation. Official prices are rigid (until another official rise), the movement of regulated ones is effectively attentuated, while contract prices keep growing. Consequently, the gap between them is continually broadening. A product sold for an official price is relatively inexpensive compared to both the costs of manufacturing (usually not covered by the price) and its utility. Products sold at free prices, as well as those sold for regulated prices, become very expensive in relation to official-priced products. This completely warps the price map, distorts the structure of consumption, prevents calculation of real labour costs and undermines the function of money as a measure of value. Even after the last rise, food, energy and services performed by the state (transport, post, utilities) were relatively inexpensive; industrial products are expensive (some very expensive indeed), and services and goods supplied by the private sector are even dearer. Milk is very cheap, supported as it is by enormous subsidies (hundreds of billions of zlotys). The price of service labour on the free market, however, is not milk but vodka-oriented!

All the authorities' announcements and programmes (for instance, the preliminary plans for 1986 and the five years 1986-1990) forecast that inflation would be down to single figures by the following year, and lower still later. An analysis of the mechanism of inflation shows that these aims were totally unrealistic, and the performance of the economy in the first half of 1985 made them more unrealistic than ever. In their efforts to curb inflation, achieve an equilibrium in the economy (which is a broader problem than the inflation itself), and get the economy or the path of at least a minimum development, the authorities find themselves between two devils and the deep blue sea. The deep blue sea is the social and economic system, inefficient, unproductive and wasteful, which, however, cannot be improved (it is unreformable) or changed lest it entail the loss of power. One of the devils is the external strain on the economy – on the one hand – the arms build-up, which includes both the current production of the arms industry and mammoth investment projects, either continuing (*Katowice* Steel Plant) or brand new ones directly or indirectly connected with it. This burden also includes costs stemming from the 'deepening integration' of Comecon, by joint investments in minerals projects in the Soviet Union. These impose burdens in the form of servicing of loans obtained from the West. But there is also a domestic devil: the resistance of workers to the attempts to shift the burden of armaments, and the system's indolence, onto their shoulders, a resistance both passive (maintaining low work efficiency) and active in the form of wage claims and threats to stop working. The soul of such resistance is of course the surviving and active *Solidarity* structures, and the moral-psychological background is the spiritual strength people gained during the sixteen months of union independence.

6. Agriculture – A Bright Spot in the Picture

An economy is such a complex system that the picture it projects is never uniform: neither completely black nor completely white. Although so far we have only perceived black areas, there are also fragments of the picture that stand out for their brighter colour. We are referring to agriculture.

Polish agriculture is an extraordinary phenomenon in a socialist economy. Three-quarters or even four-fifths of the sector consists of private peasant farms, numbering about 2,800,000. The so-called nationalised agriculture, most of it state-owned, farms 22% of arable land. Throughout the history of the Polish People's Republic agriculture has been the victim of economic, social and political discrimination and exploitation. From the moment the new system was established, agriculture was subject to two processes, both destructive: (a) economic exploitation by draining away all the economic surplus and spending it to finance industry, and (b) forced collectivisation in various forms and to varying degrees. Agriculture was always treated as an extensive development reserve from which to draw cheap labour and cheap food and in which there was next to no investment. At the same time, agriculture was, officially, the backward sector of the economy which 'did not keep pace' (with the dynamic development in industry). And within agriculture itself, the nadir of backwardness and under-development were the private farmers, always under-privileged in the sale or allocation of farm machinery and fodder, always weighed down with sundry taxes, fees, and delivery obligations greater than on state-owned farms or cooperatives.

But the Polish peasant, the private farmer, has survived. He endured the first intense wave of collectivisation of the 1950s; he endured the compulsory deliveries of the 1960s; he endured the crop and cultivation schedules imposed by local administrators in the 1970s, and resisted the crisis that struck the whole state economy, so that for the past few years agriculture has become the one hope of the entire Polish economy: agricultural production fell least during the crisis – and it was the first to regain the highest pre-crisis level in 1984, when industry was still 15% below that level. Consequently, the view was expressed more and mroe often that agriculture may become the engine of the Polish economy, and may not only pull the country out of the crisis, but also prod it forward.

It will thus be useful to realise what the agricultural miracle and its limits are. The main cause of the recent leap in agricultural production was good weather conditions which permitted big crops. The peak was 1984, with 30 quintals per hectare of the four grains, a record in Poland. This (relatively) high level of crop production creates a basis for cattle farming and the food processing industry, as can be seen from the results in the first half of 1985: the food industry was the only one in which the planned production increase was significantly exceeded and the volume of production was considerably higher than the previous year, despite the fact that the industry was subject to the same limitations (except for raw materials) as others, and its production assets wore out faster than those in other industries. It is the good results in agriculture and the food industry that brought the food market in Poland closest to being balanced, though not yet plentiful.

Together with agricultural production, the Polish farmer and the Polish village have received a boost. The peasant has gained self-confidence, and a sense of the importance of his occupation; he understands that food production is a key issue in today's world and that in this production, it turned out, in today's Poland, nobody can replace him. It is he, the individual Polish farmer driven by self-interest, working as his own boss and bearing the risk, not waiting for state planning and state subsidies, who turned the good weather of recent years into rich harvests. The fact that the socialist regime has not managed to nationalise or 'cooperatise' the body of the nation's agriculture, that it remains predominantly a private sector, is another reason for the current progress.

But it also means that the authorities' social and economic policy towards agriculture is no longer as destructive as it used to be. This policy has been sponsored by an agricultural lobby consisting of certain members of the Communist Party and the Peoples' Party. It wishes to maintain the relations between the state and indiviudal farmers on the present level, i.e. keeping social and economic conflicts to a minimum. This objective was to be served by the constitutional recognition that family farms are a permanent element of the socialist system. Let us entertain no illusions about this permanence: other clauses of the Constitution have been negated by practices that ran counter to them. But if a clause like this is backed up by a concrete political force which sees its interest in such a state of affairs, then it allows a longer-term view of the future of individual farming. And this is the way peasants perceive it. Now, in villages, brick houses are being built, investments are being made; in many areas, especially those having more fertile soil, higher culture and closer contact with the city, the outlook and pattern of living in the countryside are becoming more modern.

Also, fully equipped farm buildings, capacious barns are being erected, and farmers are investing in machinery. There is a sustained demand for tractors; individual farms possess almost 700,000 tractors, and only twice as many horses. Farmland is still in high demand; farms without heirs within the family are taken over (bought) by young individual farmers; the transfer of land to the 'nationalised' sector is minute. All this is due to the fact that farming is a paying enterprise: the remuneration is, of course, controlled by the state monopoly of supply of the means of agricultural production, machines, chemicals and construction materials, and monopsony purchase of the produce. But the farmer is not defenceless: he has kept his land, he is still the owner of the means of production. If monopoly and monopsony combined to open the price scissors, the peasant will abandon unprofitable production, cut down on purchases of capital goods from the state monopoly, reduce crops and efficiency, and return to a closed economy. Then the farmer's resistance would have to be broken by police and adminsitrative measures, instances of which have been known in history. But the Polish authorities in 1985 cannot even dream of this. It has been agreed that the only link between the individual farmers and the rest of the economy will be the economic one, and if that is to be so the farmer must be paid. And paid he is, by raising purchasing prices again and again for grains and for livestock, in the wake of (and usually with some delay) rising prices of capital goods. The farmer, of course, complains that he buys his capital goods at contract prices while selling his produce at official ones, but he keeps producing, investing, and slowly growing richer. One should realise, however, that the economic upward movement of the peasantry, of individual farming, is proceeding very slowly and reluctantly along a veritable obstacle course, the greatest hindrance being the shortage of goods to match those billions of zlotys the farmer gets for his produce. If the exchange of money for goods is difficult in the city, in the countryside it is twice as difficult. Given the shortage of goods in the retail networks in urban areas, a huge proportion of the volume of goods that reaches the peasant does so through allocation. Farm machinery, artificial fertilisers (periodically), and construction materials are all allocated, while many other goods, if not formally rationed, have to be 'negotiated'. Only a minor share of Polish industry is engaged in supplying the needs of farming. So far it has been less than 5%; 7% is now spoken about, while in the industrialised countries of the West the proportion reaches 15% or 20%. That is why the improvement in the countryside is so slow. We have mentioned that villagers are changing from wood to brick. But although thousands of new houses can be seen in the countryside, statistically the rural construction rate is low: about 50,000 dwellings a year, while the building of a single house takes five years or more, the peasant arduously gathering the construction materials after waiting to be allocated them.

Agriculture's recent success led to an increase in the sector's role in the planned export expansion. For this branch produces so-called renewable materials, and so exporting them will not impoverish the country's natural resources, as coal mining does. The shoe, it turns out, is now on the other foot: it is industry, strenuously built up for decades on the accumulation drawn from agriculture, that is not keeping up, and the engineering industry's exports are uncompetitive, and therefore good old agriculture must support it.

Still, such plans to expand agricultural exports are fraught with considerable risk. They do not take into account the fact that the present agricultural output rests on fragile foundations – mainly on favourable weather conditions, which are beyond our control. Although the productivity of Polish agriculture is now more stable than in the biblical times of Joseph in Egypt, still, even today, the fat years must be followed by lean ones and the longer the good fortune lasts, the more likely future bad crops become. How will export obligations be met then? Besides, the currrent level of agricultural production, especially that of grains, does not allow the level of food self-sufficiency needed to satisfy the population's nutritional aspirations (which involve mainly meat). To reach this, grain yields would have to rise to 40 quintals per hectare, i.e. by a third. This is technically feasible, but let us imagine that all of a sudden there is a bumper crop and we get those 40 quintals. Then two other barriers will appear which will make it impossible to make full use of the yield: the neglected state of the food-processing industry and a shortage of water. During the good results in the first six months of 1985, the food industry was running at maximum capacity and some of its branches are so obsolete that they are almost museum pieces. In the milling industry, for example, about 60% of the facilities date from the 19th century! Even now it was necessary to send Polish grain to be ground in Czechoslovakia, as it could not be done at home. In this situation, any increase in agricultural yield becomes disastrous, and reconstuction of the processing industry requires large investment which – under the existing economic strategy and system – cannot be hoped for in the next decade. So how can an agriculture and a food prcessing industry in which even packaging is an insurmountable problem become a big exporter?

The question of water in agriculture is mainly a question of animal farming. Utilising increased crop production must be reflected in livestock raising, which requires immense quantities of water. Water reaches fields in the form of rain, but cowsheds and pigsties must be supplied with it from underground reservoirs. And these reservoirs are diminishing; the Polish countryside is running out of water! Again, providing a plentiful supply of water requires heavy investment, and not just in laying pipelines. There may be faucets in villages, but no water will run from them. It is so already in many areas in the country.

The existence of the above barriers to intensive development of Polish agriculture indicates – hardly surprisingly – that it is facing rising marginal costs. This economic term means that an increment in output is more costly than the current average production cost. This means more expensive food on the nation's market, and lower competitiveness in exports. It can be seen even today in the export of sugar, from which we obtain one dollar for about 500 zlotys! Rising marginal costs in farming could be offset only by an increase in work efficiency and productivity of capital invested. This, in turn, requires that the producers having the highest costs should drop out and be taken over by more efficient producers. This would be a long process and would have not only an economic dimension, but also social and political ones. One obstacle to it is the present system of food subsidies, permitting the paying of high prices to farmers, which makes production worthwhile even for the least efficient producers. The purchasing price of milk is a notable example: consumers do not feel this high cost directly and so tend to favour the practice.

Thus at first glance agriculture stands out on the economic map of Poland as a bright spot, but an anlysis of its future prospects reveals an increasingly gloomy picture even here.

7. Investment – A Dark Spot in the Picture

There is no disagreement about the investment sphere of the economy – here everything is a uniform black. It is in investment that the gravest mistakes were made under Gierek, the greatest foreign loans were spent, the deepest slump occurred after 1980. While total industrial output in 1982 fell to 87% of the 1975 level, consumption to 84% and GNP to 76%, investment went down by 45%! This was a correct response to an economic collapse and it always happens when there is a shake-up in the economy: consumption proves to be the most rigid, the most basic magnitude, while investment is the most flexible. The point is, however, that in such circumstances there is not only a global investment cutback, but strict selection of capital construction projects, which only those that meet enhanced criteria of efficiency survive. And here we find the distinctive aspect of the problem in socialist Poland. The Gierek period left a huge mess in the field of capital investment: hundreds, thousands of projects begun, at various stages of completion, but not finished. This meant an immense freeze of capital already expended and still greater so-called engagement, or capital needed for completion. A large proportion, perhaps most, of these investments should have been abandoned. But to do this, an accurate and acceptable criterion of economic choice was needed, and no such criterion exists (no true prices and so forth). Above all, most of those projects were strategic facilities in heavy industry, the machinery industry and civil engineering, connected with or directly included in the arms programme supervised from Moscow. Could they, then, be expected to be dropped and the enormous burden of the 1970s lifted? Obviously not. There was a selection, then another, of 'continued investment projects' to decide what to halt, what to put off, and what to abandon altogether. But what should have been discontinued and what was the most costly was retained. And this was inevitable if the Soviet Union officially contracted to help the Polish People's Republic with continued investment projects in the steel industry, which permitted Szalajda (formerly the director of the *Katowice* Steel Plant, then minister, now deputy prime minister) to proceed openly with the continuation and 'stage II' of the construction of the *Katowice* works. This occupied so many construction companies that it forced a halt in, among other projects, the building of the water supply facility for Krakow, the dramatic effect of which could be seen in the ecological disaster the city endured last winter. Soviet aid with these projects amounts to supplying obsolete machinery they could not sell elsewhere, distorting the structure of the Polish economy and pushing it back into out of date technology. For their supplies, they charge us heavily, adding the cost to our constantly growing debt. In this way, their aid is in fact both an economic and a political burden.

As a result of continuing those great projects, there are no resources left for anything else. First of all, there can be no broader development of new and upgrading projects, and only the latter can start the proclaimed and expected restructuring of the economy. Then there are no funds for the absolutely necessary investments in the infrastructure, mainly in utilities, in retail trade, transport and the so-called non-productive sphere. Housing construction is restricted and declining. Gross negligence in maintenance of fixed assets is tolerated, which leads to rapid capital depreciation. Recently, under the reform, companies making profits which they want to spend on development investments, usually to modernise their plants, have come into conflict with the central planners. There have been two notable moves here by the 'centre'. In the first, the state budget took over most amortisation allowances, which in itself deprives most companies of self-dependence in reproducing their assets. In this way, the budget amasses the funds which should otherwise go to replacement investment and instead directs them to the central, continued projects. It is a policy that has always been favoured by the 'Centre'. The other moves in the financial game against the companies is cleverer; companies that undertake investment projects must make bank deposits of a certain proportion of the amount invested; the deposit is forfeit if the project does not attain its planned parameters (deadline, pay back capacity) – in practice of course it is always forfeit. The device is thus a perfidious investment tax which is aimed at discouraging companies from trespassing on the area exclusive to the centre – while supposedly respecting the principle of company's self-dependence and self-financing decreed by the reform.

As for housing, the 1985 Central Annual Plan provided for construction of 194,000 flats; it was balanced against the capacities of contractors and supplies of materials, was passed and endorsed. But right from the beginning of the year the (guaranteed!) supplies were not forthcoming to construction sites, work was behind schedule, and in the middle of the year a shortage was admitted in twelve groups of materials; as a consequence, a shortfall of more than ten thousand flats was expected.

However, what is most affected by the giant priority projects continued from the previous decade is the maintenance of hundreds of thousands of buildings and installations in the cities. Only 10% of the funds needed to prevent the progressive deterioration of these immense assets is actually devoted to their maintenance. Polish cities, therefore, are gradually deteriorating and, in some parts, going to ruin. Even many government buildings present a neglected or dilapidated aspect. In Warsaw, the capital and seat of government, the neglect of infrastructure is more pronounced than elsewhere. The heat distribution network, for example, has suffered from corrosion so much that during severe freezing weather, hundreds of houses have been cut off from heat. What maintenance of the network is actually performed is twenty times less than what is needed. The big, superbly built pre-world war I blocks of flats in the southern part of central Warsaw (Nowakowski St.) are rapidly falling into ruin, and many other famous structures, including the Poniatowski bridge and the Bristol Hotel, wait years for reconstruction which could have been avoided by proper maintenance.

When discussing investment projects, one should also consider their inflationary influence. In the Polish economic system, where there is a continual expansion of demand, a constant tendency occurs for investment projects to exceed savings; investment intentions exceed the accumulated part of income. Investment then stimulates inflation as it creates demand in the form of income for the labour employed, and does not yet produce supply to cover the demand. It is only when a project becomes a manufacturing or servicing facility that it begins to produce coverage for the previously created income and the inflationary gap is filled. If the difference in both scale and time between investment-created demand (income) and production (supply) is small, then the inflationary effect of investment is small. But if the difference and the delay are large, the inflationary gap obviously grows, unless it is compressed by income (family pay) limitations, which means increasing savings. In the Polish economy today, a major part of investment projects, including almost all the continued ones, stimulates inflation both by their long cycles and by the fact that even when completed they will not yield any increase in production. As we have seen, the population's income is not easily reduced to a degree whereby forced savings balance the investment. Furthermore, there is no unused production capacity that could, according to the Keynesian policy model, be activated by investment without disturbing economic equilibrium, for a socialist economy operates at full capacity all the time. Thus, the continued central investment projects are a powerful inflation-driving mechanism: they pump a stream of money into the economy – nearly a thousand million zlotys this year – creating nothing to cover it, and only competing against the remaining mass of currency for the still miserable quantity of goods and services on the market. Above, we described the effect of the idle sector on the labour market as a labour suction pump. Now we see the investment part of the idle sector acting on the market as a pump pouring out a stream of money. Both actions damage the economy.

8. Foreign Trade

a) Western Countries – Debts

The Polish economy does not function in isolation. The fact that there is a world economy, in which the economies of individual countries are immersed, is a great benefit for these countries as well as a challenge because it creates competition; but it can also be a trap. The Polish economy takes relatively little advantage of the benefits offered by the world economy: the volume of our exports oscillates around 10% of total social product, which is not a high level. Poland also finds difficulty competing with other economies: our products are superseded or sold below the price of corresponding goods from other exporters. Finally, Poland has fallen into the trap which the world economy can become for weak countries with lax self-discipline. The existence of an enormous world financial system which generates huge surpluses of capital gathered in banks, waiting to be invested, is an irresistible temptation for those who suffer from a lack of it. But capital alone is not enough; one must know how to invest it effectively, for only then will the loans taken become a stimulus, not a burden, for development.

Poland started to draw on the wealth accumulated in the world capital market in the early 1970s when it seemed that the abundance of capital would make it cheap, i.e. available at a low and constant interest rate. But after the mid-1970s major borrowers appeared on the capital market, including the American government, which was increasing its internal debt, and some newly industrialised Third World countires, and capital began to get more expensive. The interest rate reached 20%, which undermined the profitability even of many quite reasonable calculations. Things were made even harder for borrowers by the floating interest rate principle which means that the new price of capital applies even to loans previously extended.

If the increasing cost of capital brought headaches even to sensible borrowers operating sound economies, needless to say it was much tougher on those who spent their loans on irrational projects and then mismanaged them. Poland was the latter kind of borrower. By the end of Gierek's time in office, we had borrowed the equivalent of $20 billion. This was a sum equal, in real terms, to that received by some Western

European countries under the Marshal Plan. No detailed listing has so far been made of what those funds were spent on, but the main trends in allocation are known. One part went to investment projects in heavy, chemical, and engineering industries, including purchases of licences for these industries. Another went to grain imports to support livestock raising, which permitted increased meat consumption without higher crop production. Some of the debt simply leaked, in the form of sundry services of fealty, into the Soviet Union (this practice intensified after June 1976), some was simply wasted or stolen. These large sums were not used to redesign the structure of the economy; on the contrary, the allocation of credits was meant to reinforce the existing structure of industry. The grain imports were to provide a protective shield for the 'socialist transformation' of agriculture, the price of which would otherwise have been to perpetuate low agricultural output. At the same time, credits helped to increase consumption, which was expressed in substantial pay rises and was meant to prove that under socialism it is possible to have increasing investment and increasing consumption at the same time. The spectacular expansion of car ownership that took place then (on a Polish, socialist scale, of course) was supposed to match the population's growing income.

This fake prosperity with which the communist regime sought to bribe society toward socialism using capitalist money ended when it turned out that there was no money to pay the interest on the credits taken, let alone to pay back the credits themselves. As a result, the worst happened: new credits ceased to be given and the external reinforcement of a socialist economy by capitalism was brought to a halt. This state of affairs still continues and is the number one worry of the Polish government.

Now, five years after the collapse of the credit boom, the situation is that Poland gains one postponement of capital instalments after another as long as it pays the interest. A deal like this makes it possible to avoid declaring Poland in default, which would, of course, be very costly for our country, but also inconvenient for the world financial system. Unfortunately, the way the credit agreements or debt servicing are carried out does not remedy our position by gradually freeing us from debt; it does not even permit us to maintain our position. We pay about half of the interest due, the other half being added to the bill, which makes the debt keep growing despite the absence of new credits. During Jaruzelski's time in office it has grown by a third. One can conclude that the so-called foreign currency yield from exports to hard-currency or semi-hard-currency countries is not sufficient to cover all of the interest payments due. In 1984 about $1.5 billion of interest was paid, which consumed a quarter of hard-currency export earnings. This was thought to be the maximum permissible load on exports, since the rest must be spent on imports which are necessary to produce and, again, to export. Since the lenders agree to such servicing of the debt, the situation may be regarded as stable and treated as a permanent tax that the Polish economy has to pay to the capitalist West, a tax of about 3% of GNP. But the fact that the debt continues to grow as unpaid interest is added to the principal makes the interest grow too. In the long run therefore, the arrangement cannot be continued or the rising interest burden will crush the economy. Expert accountants have already calculated when the debt will reach $40 and 50 billion, each successive billion increment coming increasingly often, although the country, in effect, will not receive a dollar of new loans. The picture projected by such calculations cannot, however, be seriously contemplated. The economy will not bear it and this or the next governing team will itself announce the country's bankruptcy, believing that the lesser evil.

Theoretically, the way out of this situation is to increase exports to the dollar area (or cut imports) to achieve equilibrium in current transactions, so as to stop the debt from growing, i.e. pay all the interest. Since imports cannot be cut any more without damaging the exports which depend on them, what is left is increasing exports. The phrase 'Export or Perish' related to the Polish economy contains a literal threat.

A sudden leap in exports to the dollar area is quite impossible under the present system. It could only be after introducing a full market economy together with convertibility of the currency and an effective system of incentives characteristic of private ownership of the means of production. Then we could expect profitable exports to the West including goods containing less raw material and more labour and know-how, products the present state-owned and centrally-planned economy cannot even imagine. The examples of the newly-industrialised Pacific countries, Brazil, or recently even Turkey show that such an export leap, in their conditions, is possible.

With the present system, however, the economy is limited to a small gain in exports of one product group and a small drop in another, with only a slow rise in the overall surplus, too slow to overtake the growing debt. Let us see what we export to capitalist countries, and have been for years in the same proportions. Here are some 1984 data. First on the list is coal, with a share of 19%. Next are other minerals: copper, sulphur, silver, where the combined share amounted to 11%. A similar position is held by food, 10%, including meat and cattle for slaughter, which between them account for 6%. An item like down earns more than exports of agricultural and contruction machinery. Products of light industry constitute 5% of exports. Only then come ships, with 4%; vehicles and parts, 1%; lumber, 1%; and furniture, another 1%. The remaining 40% is made up of dozens of minor categories of products, mostly of a low degree of processing, among which the engineering industry, in which so much is invested, has a share, but one which altogether does not exceed one-fifth of exports to capitalist countries. This percentage also includes the export of weapons to the Third World, at least part of it for payment, but this is strictly secret and the statistics contain not a trace of information on the subject.

As can be seen, it is an export structure dominated by raw materials and food products. While the latter group can grow with the development of agriculture, the former cannot be expanded simply because it is not possible to mine more. The barrier to exporting to the West can be surmounted only by developing manufacturing industry, which, however, despite decades of investment concentrated in the engineering industry, has not yielded the anticipated results, because it is not competitive enough and offers products which are not modern enough. Not only can Poland not compete against moderately developed countries like Spain, but countries not long ago counted among the Third World also outsell us; we cannot measure up to the electronics of Taiwan, Hong Kong or South Korea.

The problems of imports from the dollar zone are less dramatic. The volume of such imports is determined by export earnings, less the necessary payments to our creditors, which, in turn, depend on the outcome of annual negotiations. Within the volume thus defined, imports are subject to strict 'rationalisation', i.e. shaping the structure to meet the needs of current production as well as possible. In this respect, the authorities have in fact followed the indications of *Solidarity's* economic programme adopted at the union's General Assembly in Gdansk in 1981, which recommended limiting investment imports to a minimum and spending the foreign currencies thus saved to import supplies for current industrial production. *Solidarity's* prgoramme anticipated – on the basis of calculations of so-called 'dollar input' efficiency and a multiplier – that this would bring about a major increase in industrial production and permit a speedy return to pre-crisis level. The results turned out to be much less impressive, but unquestionably, the clear rise of industrial production in 1983 and its further, even surprising, growth in 1984 (over 5%) is owed chiefly to directing most foreign currency earnings to imports of current supplies rather than investment goods.

b) Eastern Countries – Exploitation

Different problems are encountered in Poland's trade with the 'fraternal' Comecon countries. For both imports and exports, 60% of this trade is with the Soviet Union. From the structural perspective, we may feel satisfied with this exchange. Nearly 70% of our exports are metallurgical goods, products of the engineering industry, and chemicals – those industries, then, that made up the core of Polish industrialisation. Coal, although here, too, it is the largest single item, forms a much smaller proportion of total exports than in trade with the West and amounts to about 10%. A major proportion of exports is contributed by metallurgical products, followed by pharmaceuticals, machines, paints and dyes, products of light industry, and electronics. The last group is notable for its characteristic distribution between exports to the East and to the West: the export of computer systems to Communist countries is thirty times what it is to capitalist countries.

The structure of imports looks satisfactory, too: over 35% is fuels and raw materials (cotton). Given that the imports of gas, oil and petroleum products from this zone are three times greater than the coal, coke, and electric power exported to it, Poland is a net importer of energy from communist countries. Generally speaking, in relation to this region, we act as an economically developed country which imports raw materials and exports skilled labour. In the past, such trade with Russia enriched the Kingdom of Poland for forty years. But even though People's Poland has been trading for forty years with the Soviet Union, we are not getting richer, but, to the contrary, we are getting poorer. Where does the fault lie?

The fault lies in the fact that this socialist trade is non-equivalent; Poland's political dependence, or limited sovereignty, is reflected in the conditions and results of economic exchange. Even though the Soviet Union's role in trade with us appears to be that of a relatively backward economy, it has more than compensated for this by imposing upon us non-equivalent trade conditions. In its relations with People's Poland (and its other European satellites) the USSR has created, for the first time in modern history (it was known in antiquity), a model of colonial exploitation with a reversed flow of economic surplus: from a developed country occupying the position of a colony to a backward metropolis. The mechanism of this non-equivalence, or exploitation, is deeply concealed and cannot be seen in any statistics. Nevertheless, some of its main elements can be pointed out. The primary tool of the non-equivalent exchange is, of course, too low prices for exports and too high prices for imports, resulting from the Soviet Union's position as a monopolist supplier and a monopsonist buyer. It could be argued that monopoly and monopsony are economic terms and political dependence adds nothing new to them. But the USSR monopoly and monopsony in trading with Poland arose precisely as a result of our limited sovereignty, and then, through what in cybernetics would be called a positive feedback, it deepened our dependence while reinforcing the position of the sole supplier and exclusive buyer. Would not the use of world prices improve Poland's position? Unfortunately not. First, world prices apply only to mass, uniform goods, e.g. to coal, oil, grain, cotton, sugar. There are no world prices for industrial products for these are differentiated. This is why prices for most goods in foreign trade are settled in bilateral negotiations. Here, however, the lack of competition weakens our bargaining position with the USSR, so much that we accept unfair prices. Apart from this, in negotiations between officials, the sense of political inequality plays an immense role.

Nor are prices the only form of non-equivalent exchange; delivery conditions are another. The recipient – the vast Soviet market – dictates the time and size of consignment, threatening to cancel the deal or withhold some other supplies should the conditions not be met. The

Polish partner may, for example, have to agree to sell all of its annual production of some commodity, regardless of the situation on the home market, where there may be extreme shortage.

Another form of non-equivalent exchange is the Soviet Union's insistence on certain guarantees and manipulation of the so-called 'dollar input'. This is well known in the case of ships; Poland, as the supplier of a ship, is under obligation to repair it free of charge within the warranty period. After some cruising the ship returns to our shipyards lacking various items of equipment bought for dollars, (sometimes they have even been deliberately damaged) and we have to repair everything and replace the missing equipment under the warranty terms on which the Soviet Union insisted.

Yet another way is manipulating the quality. This concerns mass goods for which there exist world prices. Our exports are rigorously quality tested, which leads to downgrading them and thus lowering their prices. But the Soviet comrades dump sulphur-contaminated crude, impure cotton and iron ore containing clay on Poland and make us pay top prices all the same.

A new, post-crisis form of non-equivalent trade is the so-called 'service processing'. We are shipped raw material, cotton to be exact, from the Soviet Union, we spin it, dye it, weave it and sew it in our factories and return the finished product to the Soviet supplier/recipient, keeping 15% of the production. For our labour, energy, and machines which turn dirty cotton into fine shirts (containing 'dollar input, in the form of collar inserts), we receive one-seventh of what we have produced.

But the most subtle method of exploitation employed by the USSR when trading with a subordinate partner is through currency conversion. The Soviet currency – the rouble – is overvalued against the currencies of the satellite countries in relation to its purchasing power. (The dollar is overvalued, too, but this is because everybody wants to keep reserves in dollars, and besides, the dollar can always be disposed of or exchanged). The transfer rouble (supposedly convertible) is not wanted and cannot be disposed of. Its exchange rate is arbitrarily decreed and trade calculations are made at this rate.

Sometimes, however, it is effectively valued at a much higher rate. This happens with transactions (our deliveries to the USSR) where cost is difficult to determine because many elements need to be evaluated. This applies to construction assignments performed on Soviet territory. When we work on the construction of pipelines or nuclear power plants there we present to the Soviet partners our cost calculation, which of course includes particular construction conditions like rough terrain, costs of transport, additional safety devices required, and the cost of equipment imported from the dollar zone. But the Soviet side produces a calculation of its own which ignores these circumstances and shows an extremely low cost figure. On settling the accounts, it is the Soviet estimate that is binding. When we add up our costs, it appears that one rouble thus earned costs us anywhere between 300 and 600 zlotys. Our only return for carrying out such projects is a guarantee of supplies of materials, while the objects erected become Soviet property and we have to pay for actual shipments separately.

Another disadvantage in our cooperation with the Soviet Union is that it forces upon us a certain structure of investment and production which is geared to Soviet needs. Thus, we built a motor vehicle parts factory exclusively to supply the Soviet market and as a result we are tied to the Soviet monopsonist buyer. This is called deepening socialist integration!

Consequently, although in trade with the USSR Poland buys chiefly raw materials and sells chiefly processed goods, we have a steadily rising deficit on this trade. We must be processing the materials very inefficiently if we cannot earn enough to pay for them and keep something for ourselves.

c) Foreign Trade Effectiveness – How to Calculate it?

Difficulties in calculating the effectiveness of foreign trade do not concern only trade with 'fraternal' countries, but occur in all foreign trade and stem from the essence of the socialist economy. In order to calculate the effect of foreign trade one has to compare the domestic zloty cost of products exported with the foreign currency earned and then compare the foreign currency cost of imports with the zloty price at which they are sold on the home market. Only then can one compare the zloty costs of exports with the zloty revenue from imports. If the latter is greater than the former, then foreign trade is profitable and enriches the country. If the opposite is the case, foreign trade impoverishes the country, and such transactions should be ceased immediately. All this is very simple and well known to Poland's planners. The problem lies in the exchange rate between the zloty and foreign currencies. Where is this rate taken from? It is fixed by the authorities so as to cover the domestic costs of 80% of all exports. This means that 80% of exported goods have a domestic cost lower than or equal to their dollar price multiplied by the exchange rate (which, was devalued in May 1985 from 139 to 159 zlotys to the dollar). But what about the remaining 20% of exports? Why do we agree to sell abroad a 20% share of exports below cost? Surely not to subsidise foreign countries! The fact that we agree to sell 20% of exports at dollar prices which do not cover their zloty costs leads us to suppose that in reality a dollar is worth more than 159 zlotys. But how much? Unfortunately, an economic system like that in Poland cannot answer this question, for most Polish imports are not sold but are allocated administratively and their volume does not depend at all on the domestic price. The volume and structure of imports are determined by the plan. Under these circumstances, the distinction between profitable and unprofitable imports ceases to make sense. All planned imports are apparently advantageous, without distinction. In these circumstances convertibility between zlotys and dollars is out of the question. The state is unwilling to sell dollars, even at black market rates, for it is not sure if these dollars could not be spent more profitably on planned imports. Neither does the state want to sell zlotys for dollars to foreigners (to nationals, it is of course only too willing to sell them) even at a rate corresponding to purchasing power parity for this would give the foreigners a right to purchase desired quantities and kinds of Polish goods, which would constrict the central plan decisions about ther level and structure of production. Currency convertibility is thus out of the question in a centrally planned economic system in Poland or anywhere else, and official statements that such a system will be introduced 'when the economy is stabilised', or 'some time in the future'. are simply false promises designed for those who do not understand the essence of the matter.

Does this in fact cause such great economic damage? Socialist countries do somehow trade with foreign countries. Yes, they do, but it is in fact barter trade. They know that they gain in certain transactions; they can also determine certain extreme transactions which would bring a loss. But in the greater part of the trade the situation is unclear. It cannot be unambiguously determined what is profitable to export and what is profitable to sell at home, and this leads to robbing the home market of products. Nor is it possible to define what is more profitable to import with the limited means available. Thus the optimum structure and volume of trade cannot be determined, and the gains from foreign trade therefore considerably less than they would be if market principles of exchange were used. It is possible that even with the present level of trade, an increase of efficiency in foreign trade would enable Poland to earn a surplus with the Western countries, which would permit payment of all the interest due and halt the growth of the country's debt.

Part II

A PROJECTION FOR THE FUTURE

1. The 1986-90 Five Year Plan

In Part I we have reviewed the present state of the Polish economy. What can be predicted for the near and the more distant future? One attempt to answer these questions is made in the draft five-year plan for 1986-90, which was presented for public consultation. Of course, the draft was weighted down by the limitations in the vision of the Planning Committee in Warsaw, and in our thinking about the future of our economy we cannot be satisfied with that; nonetheless it is important to acquaint ourselves with the Polish authorities' thinking about the future of the Polish economy. What do they expect, what do they wish, what do they fear, what do they want to be protected from, and what do they want to do?

a) Limitations

The official documents (and there are several of them) start from what they foresee in the so-called conditions of development. Admittedly, those are realistic and even pessimistic forecasts. Thus in Poland during the next five or even ten years, there is going to be a shortage of everything that is needed for economic development as it has been understood so far, namely extensive development.

The current shortage of labour will be aggravated for demographic reasons in the next five years. The growth of population fit for employment, which is possible to calculate precisely, is going to be little more than 300,000 people, i.e. an average of 65,000 a year during the whole five-year period. In relation to the number working now this is less than one-half per cent. Labour, then, would not be a factor stimulating the economy.

There will be a shortage of minerals and raw materials for production. The increase in supplies in the next five years can be 10% at most, or an average of 1.8% per year. Coal production is expected to grow by less than 2% in the entire five-year period. Of energy sources, only brown coal and natural gas imported from the Soviet Union can expand mroe rapidly (40% and 23% respectively). Therefore the increase in electric power will be practically solely based on the mining of brown coal (with all the ecological consequences) and will not reach even 10% during the five years. The increase in most other materials from the steel, chemical, mining and timber industries will not reach 10%. Production of cement is to increase by 4% only. Imports of two main raw materials from the

Soviet Union – oil and cotton – are not expected to exceed the 1985 level.

There is going to be a lack of new machines for production. It is increasingly clear that capital asssets in the Polish economy are rapidly growing old and that the investment gap which occurred in the first half of the 1980s has delayed the possibility of replacing them, and especially of modernising the huge factories built in the 1970s. Deterioration of fixed assets threatens what some call a technological crisis, which is reflected in increasing production costs, frequent malfunctioning, declining growth of output and productivity and deteriorating quality and increasing obsolescence of products and services. If a technological crisis comes (i.e. if the phenomena described above reach a certain critical level), it is going to be considerably greater and more difficult to overcome than the production crisis of 1981-82, which was caused by a breakdown in current production processes. In order to illustrate the state of affairs, a number of figures covering the degree of deterioration of fixed assets are quoted; for example, over 59% of machines in industry are worn out. It is surprising that a very high degree of deterioration is to be found in the branches which are important for further development and enjoyed heavy investment in the past, e.g. 70% in the machine tool industry and 75% in the data processing hardware industry. Even though these are book-keeping figures (the ratio of amortisation to original value), they are nonetheless alarming.

There will be shortage of environmental resources and reserves. The present situation is described as a crossing of the ecological barrier – the limit at which the environment still has the ability to regenerate itself. Twenty-seven areas of the country, constituting 11% of its territory, but inhabited by a third of the population, are found to be in a state of ecological emergency. Rivers and lakes, as well as the Baltic coast, are polluted. Water for cities, industry, and agriculture is lacking. The air is polluted by gases rather than dust and the most dangerous among them is sulphur dioxide. It kills forests and poisons people. The soil is polluted by acid rain (dissolved SO_2 and by water drains. Polluted (acidified) soil combined with poisoned water and impure air produces poisoned food. In certain regions (e.g. in Upper Silesia and the Legnica-Glogow area) the limits of pollution considered tolerable have been exceeded many times over. And that is the state at the present production level. Any increase in production without counter-measures will accelerate the deterioration of ecological factors and ultimately retard the development of production.

And finally there is going to be a lack of foreign currencies as a result of restrictions on the supply of minerals for export and difficulties in finding export markets for manufactured products. Foreign currency difficulties will be accentuated by the need to continue servicing the debts to the West and to balance the trade deficit with the East. The lack of foreign currencies will limit the increase of imports which will, in turn, slow down the increase of production and investment, and, in consequences, of gross national product.

Being aware of the above conditions – or, in fact, limitations and even dangers – it was no easy task to create a traditional five-year plan which should be a plan of development and should forecast general growth (more and better things).

b) Growth 'Variants'

A draft of such a plan was nonetheless prepared and it does forecast growth. But it is very cautious. In order to fulfil the demands of the planning act and to conform to the 'consultation democracy' which is being introduced by the present government, the plan was prepared in three variants, from which society would choose one (?). The choice is, of course, imaginary as the differences between variants have no bearing on significant elements of economic development such as the economic policies pursued or the economic system in operation.

The starting point for the options is the rate of economic growth: lowest in option 1, medium in 2, and highest in 3. The average annual rates proposed are 3%, 3.5%, and 4% respectively. These rates are very low, compared with both past experience and 'expectations'. Why are the central planners so cautious? Because they take into account the restrictive conditions we have explained. But, even then as we will see, they do so insufficiently.

Let us look mainly at the 'middle option', No. 2, since this is the one to be adopted for implementation. Variants 1 and 3 are only meant to show possible imaginable extremes and the unpleasant consequnces resulting from them, which the moderate No. 2 will help to avoid.

The whole plan was aimed at achieving the same per capita consumption in 1990 as in 1980. This means that the plan expects the 'recovery' after the crisis to take ten years. It is, then, a very modest aim, and the fears that it will not succeed in firing the enthusiasm of the plan's main executors – the working people – are justified. It appears, however, that even as modest a target as this requires vast resources. Investment in productive fixed capital must be stepped up immediately, from 1986, to such an extent that its share in overall income must once again rise at the expense of consumption, since no foreign loans such as were received under Gierek can be expected now. The plan presents the consequences in detail: if overall income keeps growing for five years at an annual rate of 3.5%, the total increase will be 19% by 1990. Investment will then grow by 26% during the five years, or 4.6% annually, while consumption would grow by less than 13%, or 1.8% per capita per year.

These numbers contain the essence of the planned future of the economy, so, rather than provide further figures, we will have a closer look at the proposed proportions. The proportions demonstrate that the plan is designed to make a radical policy switch and half what is officially termed 'consumption growth' and what for the people is, at best, a standstill. Let us assume, however, that it will only be a slowing down of growth and consider what such growth of (per capita) consumption means. It is much less than the rate at which consumption grew towards the end of Gomulka's rule, in the second half of the 1960s, when such slow growth was considered simply intolerable. A growth rate of 1.8% annually translated into wages is imperceptible. The growth of wages was equally low in the early 1960s, but then employment grew by 3.5% a year and improved the population's overall income. There will be no such improvement now. Instead, a need will arise to improve efficiency. If the GNP is to rise by 19% and employment to remain unchanged, efficiency must grow by the same factor. How can an improvement in efficiency twice as great as the rise in pay be achieved – or, conversely, how can pay rises be held to half of the efficiency increase – in the face of a severe shortage of labour?

c) Imbalance

Such are the consequences of giving priority to investment at the expense of consumption. Let us see now if this policy solves at least investment problems. The plan assures us that the postulated productive investment will halt the decline of the capital stock 'in the sphere of material production' (i.e. mainly industry). But this is based on the premise that the value of newly built facilities will equal the value of scrapped assets. It is, then, a bookkeeper's understanding of the problem; one that is aimed at concealing the economic and technological content of the planned investment processes. And the content is this: the majority of investment in the sphere of material production is to be allocated to continuing Gierek projects. A government document says it bluntly: '..... In the first two to three years (meaning all five years) production potential will be increased mainly as a result of completing investment projects commenced in previous years.' This implies two things: first, the fall in the capital stock in industry, transport, construction and agriculture will continue (and accelerate); and second, the 'restructuring' of the economy, which would be made possible mainly by new directions in investment, will not proceed. Thus, again, immense economic effort and consumer sacrifice are to be wasted on creating and maintaining an extensive and inefficient economic structure.

Let us now consider the second part of the investment programme for the five years – investment in social consumption, which comprises housing, education, medical service and culture. The preliminary plan envisages construction of around 1,150,000 flats, or an average of 230,-000 a year. This barely exceeds the present rate, is 20% lower than the 1978 level, and is insufficient to reverse the increase in the housing shortage (at present the waiting time for a flat is up to fifteen years in big cities). Apart from that, a sum of money (620 billion zlotys) is allowed for the construction of schools and hospitals. But the programme allows nothing for the technical infrastructure and utilities which must accompany housing development. Nor are there sufficient funds for the construction of the specified number of schools needed and hospitals planned. It has been accepted that only to prevent a decline in both areas, 2,000 schools have to be built, which must cost 400 billion zlotys, and 27,000 hospital beds furnished, at a cost of 800 billion zlotys (3 million a bed). Thus, these two items alone come to double the sum provided in the plan for investment in social consumption, and yet it constitutes as much as 34% of all planned investment, which is to amount to 21% of total national product.

This demonstrates that the investment programme, despite being extended at the expense of consumption, does not solve the urgent problems of either the production infrastructure (the falling capital stock in industry) or the social infrastructure. Yet, these are not the only problems the plan must solve. Let us recall what were presented above as conditions limiting economic development. Does a plan postulating an increase in GNP by 19% in five years allow for the limitations, fit inside them, provide for overcoming them?

Let us begin with the limitations in raw materials. How can GNP (computed in material production) grow by 19% if supplies of material grow by 9%? Obviously, the consumption of materials must be reduced. And the plan provides for such savings averaging almost 9%; hard coal consumption, for example, per unit of GNP, must be cut by 14%. The imperative to economise on materials and thereby improve the efficiency of the Polish economy is right. But it must be realised that such reduction of material consumption is not accomplished by edict alone. If it were, Poland would possess the thriftiest economy in the world! Economising costs money. A reduction of 9% within five years is a huge task, especially as the Polish economy has been increasing its energy and material consumption for years. On the one hand, changes must be made in the structure of consumption; on the other, certain investments need to be made which would permit better use of materials in their existing applications. And finally, systemic changes are required to stimulate and enforce economy, e.g. elimination of marginal producers.

The plan says nothing either of investment for a more economical structure (on the contrary, it announces that for the time being there will be no change in this respect), or to reduce material and energy consumption, while it is very vague about systemic changes aimed at saving. The conclusion to be drawn from this is that the calls to economise in the plan are not accompanied by any resources to translate them into action, but are just paper regulations. Material limitations cannot be surmounted by such methods.

Nor is the plan any sounder in respect of the limitations resulting from the ecological barrier. Admittedly, it announced a policy of active environmental protection and professed both therapeutic action to reduce existing pollution and preventive action to stop it from spreading to areas not yet contaminated. But other, more sincere government declarations make it clear that the resources devoted to the task will not bring about a breakthrough. Work will continue on water reservoirs already begun – and a few others will be started – and on the few sewage treatment plants in big cities – and again, a few more will be started. Air protection, especially from sulphur dioxide, will be carried out rather experimentally, i.e. on some selected 'pilot' sites. All this is nothing new; continued at the existing pace, it amounts to cosmetic touches. Investments in environmental protection, particularly in water supply, have a long gestation period and are very costly. This is illustrated by the example of a few water reservoirs in the south of the country which have been under construction for a decade now, or that of the Water System North and sewage purification plant for Warsaw, which are now in their second decade of construction. If resources are not concentrated on ecological projects – and they will not be, for the investment allocation envisaged in the plan does not allow that – the pollution will go on spreading for the next five or ten years. The only thing that can be expected (if all goes well) is a reduction in the speed of deterioration.

The foreign currencies barrier, in relation to both West and East, is passed by in the plan with a bold announcement of an increase in exports of industrial and agricultural processed goods. Although this is technically possible, two difficulties arise: securing enough goods (e.g. coal) for export in the face of domestic demand, and finding profitable foreign markets (for food).

The above review of the basic elements of the five-year plan, which is an official projection for the future of the Polish economy, proves that the plan suffers from the fatal flaw that it is clearly imbalanced, its means do not match its end. It is imbalanced at its strategic core – in its production programme, for which the necessary energy, materials and labour are lacking. It is imbalanced at its structural core – in its investment programme, which, given the existing, acknowledged needs, exhibits a deficiency of investment funds. It is imbalanced in that the anticipated income cannot ensure the consumption, investment and surplus on trade with the West required. The imbalance in all the aspects of the plan can be summarised as an excess of demand over supply. Such a plan can be called both unrealistic (insufficient means) and not very ambitious. But then the plan is not very ambitious precisely in order to try to be realistic. If even so it is in fact unrealistic, what should it aim at to be realistic?

2. Looking for a Way Out

The five-year plan is unrealistic but this is deliberately not disclosed in the discussion in the specialist economic periodicals under the general heading 'The Price of a Perspective'. The plan's unreality, aggravated by the deterioration in the economic situation immediately before the period it covers, is a challenge for the government, which has to take action to balance the economy, for with the imbalance manifest in the draft plan the economy cannot develop, and even its current functioning, or simple reproduction, in Marxist terminology, is endangered. In this situation, the imbalance cannot help being reflected in the functioning of the idle sector*, the maintenance and development of which is a political aim and the *raison d'etre* of totalitarian rule.

Bringing the economy into balance can be achieved either by increasing the supply side or lowering the demand side. Increasing the supply side is impossible in some cases, either because of objective, natural reasons (limitations in the supply of minerals, limitations of the natural environment), or systemic reasons (determining the structure and efficiency of investment, fixed assets and production), which for the authorities are as objective as the laws of Nature. Increasing the supply side is possible, though very difficult, in other cases, such as a certain increase in the supply of labour and attempts to break through import limitations.

Greater possibilities, however, are offered on the demand side, i.e. possibilities of reducing demand. Of course, it must be done cautiously, which means selectively. For example, lowering intermediate demands (for minerals or labour) is prevented by a systemic barrier, and forcing it down would endanger production and investment. Lowering certain important final demands is altogether out of the question. This is the case with arms, strategic projects, and exports to the Soviet Union, for example. Therefore attempts at balancing have to be concentrated on final demand where there is a subjective component which is flexible and will yield to pressure by the authorities. It is easy to guess what these items are; they are the demands of the population for food, manufactured consumer goods (domestic and imported), the demand for investment in the 'consumption sphere,' for amenities etc. Here lies the main reserve for balancing the economy and improving the plan's chances of success. To use this reserve is to act in accordance with the tradition of the economic history of People's Poland, in which the population's standard of living, and especially real wages, have always absorbed the shocks of the totalitarian state's economic policy mistakes and taken second place to its priorities. Here, however, the problems of economic policy merge with the problems of politics.

Let us first see, however, what concrete actions are undertaken by the authorities to achieve balance in other branches.

Employment policy will be made more active so as to increase the supply of labour. Not only will the whole of the natural increase in the working population be mobilised, which should add some 350,000 per-

* See pp. 8, 15 and 30.

sons, but also those frictionally unemployed, which will give some 150,-000 more. To this end retired workers and women on maternity leave will be encourged to return to work, and having more than one job will be made easier. Apart from the carrot the stick will also be used. The law on 'shirkers' will be extended to cover men over 55 and to women. The labour code will be abolished in order to increase labour discipline and to increase labour intensity. Regulations will be introduced to oblige students to finish their studies on time and to take up jobs immediately upon ending their studies (and what is more limiting such employment to the socialised sector). There wil be attempts to change the structure of employment so that there will be more blue collar posts, and ensure that workers are prepared to be more flexible in the work they do.

The political effects of these changes are clear. Although wage incentives will be used, the main mechanism for achieving these goals will be compulsion. Some of the moves will be particularly drastic, for instance compulsory work for older men and women, or the introduction of high fees for students who do not take up jobs upon completion of their studies. Such steps will not increase the supply of labour noticeably, however they will create a new atmosphere in the workplace, and that is their true aim.

It is from foreign trade that the authorities expect to obtain the equivalent of increased labour supplies, and this is one of the plan's main reserves. The problem is how to increase imports from the West beyond what can be paid for by exports after the partial payment of interest on loans. The answer is simple: new loans should be obtained. An appropriate government document says: 'Financial policy... should included restoring as soon as possible full credit relations with the West and paving the way to obtaining new credits necessary for supplying production and initiating the process of modernising and restructuring productive capacity.' Now the cat is out of the bag. Now we understand why the preliminary plan did not include investment for modernising and restructuring the economy. It is the West that is supposed to supply them. This is the main reserve Poland's economy is to seek and draw on in order to 'regain the capacity for balanced development', as it is usually phrased. This is why the Polish authorities strive to win favour with the creditor banks and governments, sign agreements to defer debt payments, strain to pay part of the interest, and even make some strictly political gestures – it is all to obtain new loans on the international financial market.

Let us assume that the new loans are granted. Can they help the economy in its present situation? The economic sense of new foreign loans would be for capital in the form of minerals, materials, machines, and equipment to be made available in manufacturing to eliminate bottle-necks and cooperate with the domestic production factors and with domestic materials and energy in Polish factories, and with Polish workers, to yield a return many times greater than their cost, interest included. The effect would be reflected in a sudden leap in exports, earning foreign currency with which first to start paying the full interest on old and new debts and then to begin repaying the principal. The reasoning is logical, but we will see where the flaw is. It is where a similar calculation failed under Gierek. Gierek had everything needed for such a manoeuvre: people, materials, domestic productive assets. He did not manage to combine them effectively (i.e. quickly) with foreign capital, and then failed to sell the production thus generated profitably. Now the failure will come much sooner: there are no spare internal production factors that could be activated by foreign capital. Although production assets are not used to their capacity, the fact that machines in, for example, the textile industry work only one shift does not stem from a lack of cotton. Cotton can be bought for dollars, but there are no workers to do the spinning, weaving, and dyeing. And if there are underutilised machines and factories, they are simply not those that could produce exportable goods. Besides, when the dollars from new loans arrive, putting them to work by buying more materials will create so many bottlenecks, missing links in production, transport and storage that a new investment process will have to be started immediately. And there is no labour for that. If the machines imported in the 1970s lay idle for months because construction could not keep pace, we can imagine what will happen now. After all, no improvments have been made in the investment process.

We should realise that every dollar borrowed for production (and we assume that these loans are taken only for this purpose) entails expending ten dollars worth of domestic production factors. It is the multiplier effect at work... if there is anything to multiply.

Generally: if a country receives external capital, it must act as a complementary factor and can function productively only if manpower (and brainpower) is waiting for it, readily available. But if the labour is trapped in an existing inefficient structure, even the most abundant capital will not augment income and will either be swallowed up in consumption, or will cause additional confusion by exacerbating shortages of production factors and disrupting current production, and consequently, will generate or stimulate inflation. To expect that borrowed capital can simply substitute for a shortage of labour, or even organisation of work and economic calculation, is to dig one's own grave, politically called the debt trap. This is rudimentary economics, and we should regard this secret reserve of Polish economic development plans in this way.

Let us now discuss the main and final area where the authorities must necessarily attempt to balance the economy: the population's final demand. This demand has to be reduced; in the present economic situation; it is an absolute imperative. What is worse, the authorities imagine that this area of the economy, as opposed to foreign and strategic demands, lies within their reach and that therefore they can take decisive measures here. Recent economic performance leaves them no alternative, with production stagnating and wages and incomes generally growing, and that in real terms! According to the 1985 Central National Plan, it should have been the other way round: production and efficiency should have increased, while incomes (especially wages) should have been held down. Therefore the increase people 'independently' earned or gained in bargaining or by pressure means there can now be no question of pay rises over the five years on the scale planned in April 1985. In six months people themselves raised their wages by half of what they were supposed to get during five years. That is the truth. From this the authorities must draw conclusions.

3. A Possible Scenario

In the immediate future widespread actions will be taken to try to reduce the population's demand, i.e. to cut income intended for current consumption, and to limit investment in consumer goods and services. There are several ways of doing this; nominal incomes can be controlled – they can be frozen or even reduced, prices can be raised quicker than nominal income, reducing real income. Indirect taxes can be levied or increased, which is a slightly subtler method than direct reduction of income by various dues or direct taxes. It is a variant of raising prices, in fact. Not all the measures taken will necessarily apply to all groups of the population. Action may be selective.

The operation of reducing the population's demand is a difficult one for any government, even a totalitarian one; the problem is to minimise both the economic and especially the political costs of the operation. In Poland, an operation of this kind was performed at the beginning of the martial law period, in February 1982, when prices were doubled while nominal income increased one and a half times. But then the authorities held the whip hand: the people were surprised and frightened. Today the method of hitting everybody at the same time has to be avoided if possible, because it could disturb the political process of normalisation. The authorities must also try to prevent the reduction of demand from having repercussions on production, for this would lead to a drop in supply and delay rather than speed up the regaining of balance.

The above principles show the direction of attack; the victims will be those social groups which are either professionally passive, or do not have sufficient production self-dependence to react with economic resistance. Thus we can presume that the operation will spare individual farmers, and also, which may appear incredibe – the so-called extra-agricultural private sector: small business. This group, which is of course condemned to extermination by official doctrine, has not yet fulfilled its task of saving the socialist economy, and if we apply the model of the Soviet NEP we shall see that its time has not yet come.

Who is left then? The increasingly numerous pensioners. Despite numbering about six million, they are socially a weak group. Their reactions to the restrictive measures will not be reflected in supply for they do not produce anything. The authorities need not fear their political resistance. That stems from the state of psycho-social insecurity of people not engaged in professional activity (this is a common phenomenon, not only Polish). Although pensioners have been the group most affected by diminished incomes during the crisis, as a group they do not offer any resistance; on the contrary, they want stabilisation and are a pillar of 'normalisation'. Their sense of insecurity tells them that any greater disturbances in the social order can only worsen their lot.

Finally, there are the employed workers, the most numerous group who also have the biggest share in consumption. From the point of view of the ability to resist the expected economic restrictions, this group cannot be treated uniformly. The employees of the so-called non-productive sphere do not count in the calculation. Their work serves predominantly the people, so even if they do disrupt the rhythm of work or cut down their efficiency, it will not show in the balance of the economy. Apart from that, members of this group are scattered, and so unlikely to put up organised resistance. They can be struck with impunity.

It is different with the workers in the production sphere, those employed in industry, construction, and transport. The experience of the *Solidarity* period showed that they are the core of the working class capable of organising resistance against the 'class of trilords' (to use the term coined by Leszek Nowak). Their resistance may prove effective especially in industry and transport, where it will slow down production and upset the current functioning of the economy. In construction the problem is somewhat different, as the sector does not produce immediate output effects.

But the group of employed workers, even those from big factories in the production sphere, has a significant weakness in displaying its resistance: they are not owners of the means of production as farmers and craftsmen are, they are not independent manufacturers and thus they do not command their products. Employed workers cannot therefore abandon producing; they can only stop temporarily and then – even after a year-long strike, like the British miners – they have to return to production as this is their station in the social division of labour. Therefore their resistance can only have an organisational-technical, never an economic character. The awareness of this deficiency during the *Solidarity* period stimulated the union to look for another form of resistance, an 'active' strike consisting in appropriating the product, but it failed to do this, of course.

Therefore, despite employed workers, as opposed to pensioners', ability to organise resistance, it is they who will be the chief target of the authorities in their attack on demand. Another reason is that they are the main driving force of the population's consumption and income claims, and destroying this force would stop the whole process.

How will it be carried out? First, wages must be frozen. In the present economic situation, this is an absolute necessity the authorities are facing; it simply stems from the laws of economics – virtually as binding as those of Nature. A wage freeze (even now reducing nominal wages is out of the question; the only possible movement of nominal wages is upward) is an operation more difficult to perform than price manipulation, more brutal, and aimed at concrete people, but it cannot be avoided. It is only when wages are frozen (and thus the increase in the income of other groups is halted or slowed down), that it will be possible (and necessary) to turn to price operations. The three general price rises of recent years, including the largest in 1982, were immediately counterbalanced by a strong upward wage movement. Raising prices when wages are mobile is like trying to fill a leaking pot. The leak must first be plugged, i.e. wages frozen. This has to be the authorities' line of reasoning. The price changes which will be necessary will prove much more severe than the rises in 1984 and early 1985, as this time no pay rises will absorb the shock. Things like meat rationing, for many a nuisance, will become a minor issue. All of society's conscious thought will be occupied by the new phase of struggle to maintain the existing standard of living. In order to curb the growing current of wages which flows into factories, offices and institutions the authorities will have to adopt the so-called hard financing and introduce financial discipline to the extent that banks can and do withhold the money to pay wages (in individual, albeit not so rare cases). They will also have to cancel or at least limit drastically the various pay entitlements which cause a heavy outflow of money from December to February every year: bonuses and 'profit sharing' that are paid regardless of the actual financial situation of a company, the market and the economy.

Simultaneously, measures must be taken on the price side of the equation. For the time being, food prices will probably not be the scene of the assault. Both good crops and the fact that increases in food prices always excite the strongest response make this unlikely. On the other hand, the temptation, or even intention, to make agriculture and the food industry export champions may prompt a removal of more food from the domestic market and its shipment abroad. There may also be heightened demands from the East. All this can be carried out by means of a price increase. Food prices are still relatively low (compared to industrial products), while the huge subsidies are a heavy burden on the budget. It is plausible to assume, however, that at the first stage, food prices will be left alone. But new prices of energy and fuel will begin to be felt, and further rises cannot be ruled out (they remain far below cost); there will be (must be) an increase in train and bus fares and postage, although perhaps not as much as to eliminate subsidies (a bus ticket in Warsaw would then have to cost 15 zlotys). And finally, rises will extend to rents and members' contributions in housing cooperatives

Here, the gap between prices currently paid and costs incurred or costs of wear and tear is the greatest, while the population's mental preparedness for increases is the least. For forty years, the Polish people have got used to low fares and the Communists deliberately pursued a policy of freezing rents on flats and appropriating them without payment, which permitted wages to be kept low, as the amortisation costs of housing inherited from the pre-war period were financed from the grave by the 'rugged burghers', tenement owners who had built the houses prior to 1939. Now that housing built after the war prevails, the question of deterioration – and thus financing repairs – has made a conspicuous appearance. Housing in Polish cities deteriorates rapidly since there is insufficient funding for maintenance and repairs and soon the extent of necessary demolition will match the number of newly built flats. So far, these expenses have been covered, though insufficiently, by the budget. Now the budget must be relieved of some of this burden, while expenditure must be increased; the funds must then be found in what has so far been wages. Just how big a rise in rents is necessary to balance this segment of the economy is indicated by the (inadequate) budget subsidies for housing, which are now 10 zlotys per square metre per month, while rents paid are between 10 and 25 zlotys per square metre per month. Rent now amounts to 3% to 8% of family budgets, while a full charge would boost this proportion to up to 20% of total household expenditure.

Still more difficult is the issue of paying for new house building. Costs of construction (by the state) are growing much faster than inflation and today are about 40,000 zlotys per square metre, which means that an average flat (50 square metres) costs 2 million zlotys. Raising the tenant's contribution even to as little as 30% of this figure would equal thirty months' average pay.

The conclusion to be drawn from this is that any significant reform of rents and construction financing must shake family budgets considerably more than the recent, selective food price increases, all the more so since housing needs are inflexible in the short run and expenditure on housing is not easily escaped.

Price regulation will probably be topped off with a rise in the price of alchohol and especially cigarettes, which are still relatively inexpensive in Poland. These official price increases will be followed by a wave of contract price increases, in efforts to catch up with the official price index.

The whole massive and inevitable price operation would not be so severe for the population – and particularly for the recipients of wages, pensions, and benefits – if it were offset in the way it was before in such circumstances by an appropriate increase in wages, etc. But if the operation is to bring real changes in the distribution of GNP and curtail the share of consumption (and this is the point), there can be no compensation, or at least the government will do all it can to prevent it.

In order to improve the chance of success, the authorities will have to mount a propaganda campaign, which will take the form of 'a moment of truth' about the economy. People wil have to be told what the economic situation really is, that the crisis is deepening and becoming permanent, instead of spreading illusions about the 'light at the end of the tunnel'. There will be no room for the half-truths of optimistic media commentators like: 'the situation contains optimistic elements and the crisis is going to last for another year at most.' People will have to be told bluntly: 'Citizens, we are still living beyond our means and this cannot go on any longer'. It will be true, but not the whole truth, for the people of Poland are living beyond their means because we are putting a great part of our social energy into the idle sector, from which nothing returns to the economy. This being so, it really is impossible to sustain the current standard of living.

Of course people are going to ask why the crisis is prolonged and even deepening. The government's moment of truth will not, however, go that far into the actual reasons for our economic collapse, and thus will not manage to disarm society morally and politically and win any confidence for a policy demanding new sacrifices from the population, if only because it will not be able to promise anything. A moment of truth must send powerful shock waves through society, but the shock will not be favourable for the authorities. The authorities' partial candour will not build confidence in the government, the economic leadership, the system; on the contrary, it will help unveil the depth of the crisis and undermine the authorities' present frail legitimacy based on assurance that things are improving a little. The only likely social response will be resistance. But since the authorities have no choice but to carry out such an operation, a struggle is going to ensue. How fierce it will be and who will win will depend on the strength of society's resistance on the one hand, and the determination of the government and its apparatus on the other. Four times in the history of the Polish People's Republic the authorities retreated when confronted by society: in 1956, 1970, 1976 and 1980 (in the last case without a fight). The fifth time round (December 1981) it was the authorities who launched an attack and won an easier victory than either camp had anticipated. What is it going to be like next time?

The strength of the authorities' attack will depend on their determination and this, in turn, will depend on their assessment of the situation and the uniformity of views in their ranks. In the assessment of the situation, the most important factor is their judgement of the economy, and this is an element that can strengthen their determination. Here, the authorities have nowhere to retreat, they have their backs to the wall. This time the Communists appear to command no political reserves as they did in 1956, 1970 and 1980. Political self-confidence stemming from victory in the price confrontation on 1 July 1985 might also be a factor in their determination. But this tends to be transformed into conceit and arrogance, which will work against them.

Of course the authorities are not going to confine themselves to an operation affecting pay and prices, and adminstrative and possibly police action. They will also launch a propaganda campaign to divide and antagonise society internally. The main points of such a campaign have been used many times: slogans about fighting income inequality, excessive amassing of riches, profiteering and social parasitism. In particular they will try to drum up hostility toward private entrepreneurs and farmers. It is always easy to use the argument that the peasantry is getting rich at the expense of the working class, which undermines the 'worker-farmer alliance' and 'income parity'. On top of this, there will appear (are already appearing) suggestions to the effect that private farming is inefficient and, considering the Czechoslovakian and Hungarian examples, the issue of its 'socialist transformation' should be revived.

And what about the other side, society? Who and what can we count on? The peasantry will not stir, at least not at the initial stage of the conflict. Not directly attacked *en masse*, it may rise to some gestures of solidarity, but in principle it will be endeavouring to sit out the storm. The same can be said about the private extra-agricultural sector. This group may yet become a political force, but only later. At present most of them face the authorities, and particularly the department of finance, individually. Pensioners – although they will be the most affected by the economic restrictions and pushed down to a yet lower level of existence – will not budge.

There remains employed labour, especially workers and technicians in big companies, mainly people between twenty and forty years of age. There are 2 million of them and this group can be organised to offer resistance. In this group we can distinguish those whose discontent and demands are particularly strong. They are women working in big factories where they constitute a majority of employees working in close association. Women earn less than men, they bear the burden of housework, and they are the first to face the difficulties of everyday life which are so irritating in Poland. They also feel most acutely the growing costs of living and the shortages on the market. The next riot by Polish workers may well be started by women – a new kind of shock troops of workers' 'counterrevolution'.

The organisation of social resistance has to start with and consist chiefly in rousing people's awareness. Of course, the technical aspect of resistance is important, but rousing awareness is of fundamental import. Society lost on 13 December 1981 and during the following, decisive two to three weeks not because it had technically weak means of struggle; what was weak was its determination, a certain state of awareness. What is needed to rouse awareness is a team of activists who themselves have a programme able to point to and, first of all, identify both the immediate and long-term interests of workers. Here it becomes apparent how important the fact is that *Solidarity* structures and activists still exist, and although they are weakened, decimated, and marked by failures, they are not vanquished or politically disarmed. This fact means that in the approaching confrontation, the authorities do not necessarily have to be the winner.

In preparing the awareness and readiness for social resistance, *Solidarity* will not start from scratch. It is true – and has been repeatedly emphasised by underground writing – that the Polish society of 1985 is not the same as that of 1975; that the sixteen months of *Solidarity* and then four years of opposition press and literature have developed social awareness, so that Polish society today is – like Marx's class – not only a 'society in itself', but a 'society for itself'.

But it is not enough. It is not enough for people to have a general knowledge that the situation is bad and not improving, contrary to what is announced by official propaganda. It is not enough for them to know that their misery is caused by the system of government, economic policy, or even simply socialism. In order to organise social resistance and develop the necessary psychological and moral determination in people, their concrete and current interests have to be articulated and they have to be convinced that passivity inevitably endangers these interests. People must be persuaded that resistance, together with the costs the fight entails, will be a lesser evil than passive acceptance of growing pauperisation. And they will be persuaded when they are shown the mechanism which necessarily leads our country and our economy from bad to worse. This mechanism is the constant growth of the idle sector in the economy, a parasite feeding on the productive parts of the system like cancer, and there is no limit to this process unless it is stopped by the people themselves. Any savings achieved at the expense of our consumption, any profit which amounts to our being exploited, any rationalisation, improvment in efficiency, streamlining, will be funnelled into the idle sector for its enrichment and development. For the authorities, the real cost is our consumption – consumption by labour – and it is this they desire to minimise.

Therefore our economy is rapidly sliding down in a diminishing spiral. And it is an illusion that the slide will stop when we reach the bottom. There is no bottom (it has been stolen – a black joke has it). The only bottom can be peoples' resistance. We have to persuade ourselves and others that there is no other way out.

In order to strengthen the attitudes of determination that will enable people to resist, the moral aspect of the action should be explained. It is a terrible truth that things must get worse in order to get better. However, it should be understood that passivity and failure to oppose evil are morally to be condemned, and not only the oppressor but the oppressed too are guilty if by their passivity they encourage and even justify evil ('if they take it quietly, it must be right'). It will not be possible to organise social resistance effectively under petty slogans. The demand for a cost of living supplement is all very well as a first step. But because it certainly will be disregarded by the authorities, the struggle has to be for the essential things, i.e. for everything. At the same time, mumbling about 'agreement' should be stopped as it causes confusion and creates the illusion that there is another way out.

4. The Unusable Reserve

Let us stop this dangerous scenario of possible future developments and return to strictly economic matters. The crisis of the Polish economy stems from two sources: from a specific economic policy maintaining and developing an idle sector, and from an economic system which causes the economy to operate extensively, and thus inefficiently, with excessive consumption of raw materials, energy, capital and labour. If pursuing this specific economic policy is an exogenous element for the authorities, which they take for granted and cannot change even if they wanted to (assuming they were able to want to), then why do they not introduce changes in the functioning of the system to make it work more efficiently, so that economic policy would be more effective and the idle sector would receive more from the economy. Why do they not try to 'do a bad thing well' (i.e. more efficiently)?

Well, they do try and this is what the reform is all about. But, as is widely known, the reform is a failure, it is ineffective. The decision makers want the results expected of the reform, but they do not want the reform itself; they do not want to pay its social and political costs. Therefore, individual changes in the so-called system of control are introduced superficially, inconsistently, and with exceptions which are so numerous they constitute a rule, are suspended for the sake of 'temporary', pre-reform solutions, and, above all, do not tackle the most important problems of the system: the market and control of the means of production. Why is this so? Why do the authorities refuse to pay the costs of reform if it would allow them to carry out their present economic policy more efficiently? The answer is simple: they could not. System of functioning and economic policy are closely connected, like means and ends. This economic policy, the maintenance and development of the idle sector, could not be sustained with a different system of functioning.

Is the system reformable at all? No, the system can only be changed. And the economic policy with it. We must realise that it is not going to be a simple process and then, too, a price will have to be paid. The price will be abandonment of the socialist style of work. To get the country out of the crisis and out of poverty in general, after the destruction inflicted on it by the system of real socialism, the people must get down to work. The Communists offered society the implicit deal: 'Let us rule, and we will let you work little and poorly'. It meant corrupting the people to tolerate a totalitarian regime. Democratic government will have to reverse this and say: 'If you want us to rule, you will have to work for it'.

Part III

A YEAR LATER

A fresh look at the Polish economy a year later enables us not only to update the economic picture of the country, but also to draw comparisons between the situation observed at two different times and so to see the trends. We can also check our previous assumptions and scenarios.

1. The Current Situation

a) Production

We will begin, as we did a year ago, with production. The traditional GUS announcement, 'On the Country's Social-Economic Situation in the first half of 1986' provides the traditional information: how much was produced, how much sold, how much transported, how much money people earned and how much they spent. But despite this hackneyed form, it is an astonishing announcement: nearly everything is repeated, though against a somewhat different background. In 1986 there was no mysterious economic break-down during the winter months as there was in 1985, although winter was hardly less severe. This resulted in a relatively sharp increase in industrial production indices in the early months of 1986 compared with the low level of the previous year. However, this particular 'benefit' begins to disappear as we leave the first months of the year behind us and begin estimating the industrial production increase in relation to the level of the summer months in 1985. Then, the high growth figures of the first quarter – 6.7% and even 9% for corresponding periods, give way to much smaller figures in the second quarter: 3% in April, 3.7% in May, and in June, over a corresponding number of working days, there was a 2% decrease in production.

And so, again, there is a declining curve, this time in a monthly sequence. It can be expected that the indices for the second half of the year will be still more modest.

We should bear in mind that the high growth rates in the first months of 1986 are, in the majority of cases, an illusion. Since in the first half of 1985 there was no increase – indeed even a decrease – in production in relation to 1984, the 1986 figures should be treated as illustrating growth over two years, i.e. in relation to 1984. If we calculate them in this way, they will show little or no progress. This is clearly demonstrated in the production of separate groups of products which are estimated in natural units. For pig iron, the growth index for the first half-year of 1986 is 108.9, but, in the first half of 1985 it went down to 95.6; thus progress in relation to 1984 is 4.3%. It is still more striking in the nitrogenous fertiliser industry: the 1986 index is 131.2, but the growth in relation to 1984 is only 3.2%, an annual average of about 1.5%.

Apart from that, in some important groups of products we can even observe a drop in production in relation to the peak year of the 1980s – 1984. The production of cement – to use the familiar example – was more than 11% lower in the first half of 1986 than 1984, production of plastics was 6% lower, natural gas 3.7% , petroleum (processing) 0.3%, rolled steel products 1.5%, refrigerators 2%, farm machines 3%, sulphur 5% and synthetic fibres down 0.7%. There was a spectacular breakdown in the production of synthetic rubber and tyres: down 7% even from the first half of 1985. As regards foodstuffs, the production of butter decreased by 15.5% and the fish catch by 18%. In both cases this was also a decrease in relation to 1985. Finally, production of coal was nearly 1 million tons less than two years before, in the first half of 1984. Even worse than production was the market supply of certain groups of goods. Compared with the first half of 1985, supplies of refrigerators and TVs were 5% less, cloth almost 10%, knitwear more than 4%, and clothing as much as 8%.

The above figures show that industry has clearly entered the phase of stagnation. In some branches, in some product groups, production is still increasing thanks to special mobilisation and concentration of resources, but in others, despite great efforts, there is stagnation and sometimes a sudden slump. This destroys material balances, causes confusion with sub-contractors, gives rise to numerous bottle necks and forces industry as a whole, together with the entire economy, to work at maximum capacity without reserves that could lift it out of stagnation or insure against further collapses.

This situation in industry is projected onto the construction sector too. Its performance in the first half-year was even worse than in industry, as construction functions particularly inefficiently in this system. In the first half of 1986, construction hardly grew at all in relation to the year before, and in the last month of that period, June 1986, was nearly 10% lower than in June 1985. The building breakdown was felt most by that part of the sector which is particularly socially important and is countable in physical units – housing. In the first half of 1986, 7% fewer flats were completed than in the same period a year before. The extent of fulfilment of the annual plan in this sector (which is very modest in any case) in the first half-year was 33%, an extremely low figure which was also less than in the preceding year.

b) Coal

We previously pointed to two (out of many) causes of Poland's economic languor. Both are at work today, too. The first is the coal, or more broadly, the energy situation. There has been no improvement since a year ago: there is no more coal, and specific consumption is growing no less rapidly. Therefore, if production in one coal-using branch is to expand, coal consumption must be limited elsewhere. Thus coal-guzzling cement plants have been closed down, and cement exports reduced, hurting hard-currency earning ability, supplies of coal to agriculture have been cut, and attempts made to limit coal consumption throughout industry (though ineffectively). The result is another brake on industrial growth, and, indirectly, on the whole economy. One of the causes of poor results in construction is a permanent lack of raw materials, particularly of cement. There were problems with cement last year, but what was then scarcity could be called abundance today.

c)Labour and Wages

The other cause of the paralysis of production is the lack of labour. There has been no improvement here either, indeed the situation has got even worse. Employment offices offer half a million jobs to a few thousand candidates. At the same time, hundreds of enterprises and institutions advertise, nearly begging people to join them. As the response to those pleadings is faint, sections of factories are closed down, shifts are limited, production and services reduced, and hours of work lengthened by various means (e.g. by the so-called economic teams). The difficulties factories face are less visible to the outsider, but what is happening in trade and services directly affects people: like a year ago, many shops are closed, opening hours shortened, post, railway station, and bank counters are unstaffed. We discussed the causes of this state of affairs before. Now we can add that another year of the mock-reform has brought no changes in labour management, nor has it revealed any reserves, in short, it has not intensified employment. However, it did bring certain, though not quite expected results: for instance, state utilities are losing people from maintenance groups, and then the same people – as employees of private firms – are hired by state municipal institutions and do the same maintenance – but now at different pay rates and on a different basis.

Speaking of pay rates we have touched on the problem of wages. As we know, lower wages do not encourage people to work in the state-owned sector, and especially in services. In order to counteract this, the management in state enterprises and many institutions follow a flexible wages policy: they agree to wage rises, or even initiate them, which coincides with the pressure exerted by the ranks of workers in big enterprises. There has been no change here. Company wage systems, which were supposed to have introduced discipline, had the reverse effect, becoming a means of further leniency. Average industrial wages in the first half of 1986 were 21% higher than in 1985, the identical increase as that in 1985 in relation to 1984. In the last month of the half-year there was a new acceleration; wages in June 1986 were 23% higher than a year before, whereas the corresponding figure in June 1985 was only 17%. As we have said, wages, being the fundamental part of the population's income, influence the remaining kinds of income, i.e. social benefits and individual farmers' incomes. The population's income in the first half of 1986 was nearly 23% higher than in the first half of 1985, whereas the planned increase was only 15.5%.

d) The Market

Price movements were supposed to be controlled so as to ensure the planned real income. The GUS announcement does not say a word, however, on the subject of prices and costs of living, nor does it specify sales of goods and services by value or volume. From this source, therefore, we cannot infer whether the market is approaching stability or whether it has moved further away from it. On the basis of our own ongoing 'participant observation' as buyers, we have noted two tendencies in the movement of prices: free market prices, especially food prices, followed the increase in incomes smoothly, ensuring balance between supply and demand, whereas state market prices rose by leaps, with a prolonged period of freeze being followed by a jump of 50-300% (city transport fares for example). On the other hand, the state market in manufactured goods remained, as in previous years, in a state of deep disequililbrium, the majority of product groups displaying enormous gaps in supply and a lack of continuity in sales. But in the case of some products (e.g. carpets) a GUS announcement for the first seven months of 1986 speaks of growth of retail stocks by one-third compared with 1985. Unfortunately, the goods concerned are unwanted, so this is hardly a cause for satisfaction.

Generally, the state of the market testifies to a persisting deep gap between the structure of production and supply and that of demand. The economic reform ostensibly in operation since 1982 has not brought any improvement in this field, while the appearance of Polish-foreign companies and the gaining of a higher proportion of the market by private enterprise have managed no more than a marginal enhancement of market supply. (The quality of this production is in any case generally low and the standard of design of private manufacturers deplorable).

The population's financial resources, on the other hand, are growing month by month. In part they are regular savings made voluntarily. But most constitute the so-called inflationary overhang waiting to be spent. The population's total financial resources in mid-1986 were about 3 billion zlotys, or some 45% of its annual income. This is not high for a normal economy, but with the production structure in Poland this sum cannot be spent on goods or services. The Polish economy caters predominantly for current survival, for people to last the month, not producing sufficient quantities of durable or even semi-durable goods. Thus, 15 to 20% of people's monthly income is saved and this constitutes at least 70% of the inflationary gap, which is what creates the growing excess purchasing power. This overhang phenomenon in itself – the slowing down of the velocity of circulation and growing accumulation of currency – is nonsensical with an annual price inflation rate of about 20%, as in real terms the savings melt away at an exponential rate. The overhang is simply a debt owed to society by the state, and the effect of inflation is to ease this burden. If the people still go on 'lending' the state 15 to 20% of their income, it is because they cannot help it, they cannot find anything to buy with the money.

e) The Problem of Equilibrium

The problem of inflationary gap and inflationary overhang is characteristic of socialism and results from a lack of equilibrium on the market. In market economies even three digit inflation does not lead to any overhang; there is no problem in spending money as goods (at equilibrium prices) are waiting for the consumer. Therefore, there have been repeated calls to change Polish price policy and let prices maintain balance between supply and demand on both the consumer and procurement markets. Of course, we are in favour of equilibrium; it is a normal state for an economy. But superficial transfer of isolated elements of a market economy into a socialist system will not do. Let us assume that prices are raised to a level at which they will balance the exsting supply with demand. Only demand will then respond: marginal buyers will be eliminated and queues will disappear. But the supply side will not respond: higher prices, and hence extra profits, will not lead state manufacturers to increase supply because they will not be allocated additional means of production, their profits will inevitably have to be paid into the budget in the form of taxes and, as monopolies, they are not going to be interested in expanding their output.

In any case, even if balanced markets were achieved, the balance would be threatened by an inevitable expansion of demand from many directions. This is because market equilibrium assumes, by definition, plentiful supply: goods waiting for buyers. The sense of plenty (but at fixed prices and with buyers' existing income and preferences) will lead to increased demand: if the goods are there, why cannot they be bought, why cannot people earn more to buy them, why cannot additional investment be made to put these machines and materials to use, why cannot this 'surplus' on the market be exported? With such unlimited creation of effective demand as occurs in the socialist economic system, one can be sure that the apparent surplus of supply over demand which exists at equilibrium prices will soon be taken off the market and imbalance will reappear, to be corrected by another price increase. This mechanism is simply trivial and has been observed many times. There has never been lasting balance on the basic markets in the economy in People's Poland. Such classical equilibrium occurs only on markets dominated by private manufacturers, and those who suffer no great restrictions on access to production factors, such as the markets for vegetables, fruit and eggs – products with a low income-elasticity of demand and limited export opportunities. Yet if, for example, in the Soviet Union a new policy now aims at expanding the volume of goods on their market and a Soviet delegation comes to see our orchards and fruit processing plants, we can confidently expect the (relative) abundance of produce on these markets to dwindle, and equilibrium to disappear there too.

Market equilibrium requires not only prices that balance supply with final demand. It also means equilibrium prices at all the preceding stages of production, including for factors of production, the curbing of monopolies, competition between manufacturers (retailers) and, most important, a different allocation of factors of production and of the goods and services produced in all stages of the economic process. On a balanced market goods and services will go to the buyer who has the money, and the goods that will meet his demand are the ones that will sell.

f) Investment

An economic equilibrium thus understood must also shape both the volume and structure of investment. The reality in our economy is, however, entirely different. Investment is the weakest link in the Polish economy in respect of both its allocation and the efficiency of the investment process. The latter is exemplified by the lengthening investment cycles which add to the burden on the economy, tying up more and more resources in unfinished projects. In 1985 the planned completion of investment projects was fulfilled by only 65%, four points below the 1984 level.

It is sometimes asked why, despite the crisis the economy is in, the authorities and companies not only keep investing, but aim at increasing investments. Since 1983 capital expenditure has been growing, not only in absolute terms, but also in proportion to GNP. We partly answered this question in Part I; now we will supplement that discussion. In a centrally planned economy with predominantly state-owned means of production, there is a strong tendency to continuous expansion of investment. Now, after a few years of lower capital expenditure, the policy of increasing it has been revived; the preliminary plan for 1986-1990 promises to continue and reinforce this trend, though of course not on the scale of the 1970s, when domestic capital spending was augmented by huge foreign credits.

There are various motives behind forcing capital investment. The general reason for the phenomenon is the constant expansion of demand which gives economic agents – companies, budget institutions, and the population – financial resources in relative abundance at all times, and indeed, in excess of the availability of goods; this makes it possible for spending to grow and, on the othe hand, encourages a belief in capital spending as a way to preserve the value of these resources.

Superimposed on this general tendency to invest are particular reasons and impulses of investors. The central authorities, which are the main driving force behind the process and have the most resources at their command, have several reasons for maximising investment. The main reason is to create power to strengthen their rule over society. This power is created, socialist decision makers intuitively feel, by capital goods such as new coal mines, steel plants and factories, preferably in the engineering industry. These are supposed to serve the role played in the Middle Ages by the castles and palaces of feudal lords: they are to be the forge of the socialist authorities' strength, and spending on such projects should reach the limits of possibility (and beyond). Another motive is the economic doctrine which proclaims that capital investment is the main – and in the long run the only – factor ensuring economic growth, which, in its turn, is necessary to build external strength to compete with the capitalist world. In addition, investment projects are needed by the central planners to ensure full employment.

Companies have more prosaic (though similar) motives for expanding investment. They invest to enlarge their plants and so boost their prestige. Investing is also a relatively easy way to meet production plans. Another factor is the weak, or non-existent, link between investment and plant operation, because of which difficulties in the latter are no hindrance to the former.

Investment impulses in the so-called budget or non-productive sphere are similar to what they are in the non-socialist world, in which budget officials think along similar lines (and make similar mistakes). Here, too, the point is to obtain the greatest possible funds for one's institution or region to be spent on investing in infrastructure projects as needs in this domain are, as everywhere else, always great.

Finally, one more factor to encourage investment is demand created within the investment process itself: it causes industrial bottlenecks to appear and overcoming these needs further investment. This is a self-perpetuating process, of course.

An additional personal motive is that people engaged in investment projects derive extra income from them, in the form of bonuses, higher salaries, perquisites – all these are more easily obtained from investment projects than routine production.

All these motives and factors, however, would not be sufficient to sustain the continuous investment pressure if it were not for an additional factor which fundamentally differentiates socialism from capitalism. Namely, in socialism, capital investment decision making does not involve the question of cost. Of course, there is expenditure, there are costs to pay, but the decision making agent does not perceive these costs as something that shoud be more than compensated by revenues. This perception is encouraged, among other things, by the time interval between making the expenditure and obtaining production effects from the project. And if there is no cost, then there is no risk of a failed investment. On the contrary, investment decisions are always taken with confidence that some greater or lesser benefit will result. And the feeling is basically right, for if the resources invested are costless to the investor, then the final result is most likely to be favourable.

This fact, in turn, obviates the need to make calculations – no thought is given to the project in terms of cost efficiency and anticipated revenues. With major investment decisions, the central planners do not even attempt to calculate cost and profit. Although companies perform some calculations of their own according to the accepted methods of capital accounting (there are special instructions on the subject), their results are not treated seriously, and rightly so: the false prices used in the calculations makes them worthless. Still, one might think that companies would consider the cost of (lost) opportunities as they after all tie up their own resources, at least in part. But, first, these resources are not quite their own – one of the reasons being that a company's capital spending is partly financed by bank credit to be paid back in the distant future, beyond the perspective of the current board of directors – and, second, the cost of (lost) opportunities is little or none as the profit can be taxed away into the state budget. As a result, the best thing a company can do with a surplus is to invest it. In the case of budget-financed institutions, the situation is even simpler: investment is financed solely from subsidies, and so even formally it is free.

In these circumstances, investing does not involve risk or economic responsibility. No one has yet gone bankrupt in a socialist economy because of a miscalculation or mismanagement of investment. And when hundreds of billions of zlotys sunk in projects during the Gierek era had to be written off, nobody bore political responsibility for those mistakes. Thus investment decisions in the socialist economic system do not depend on the current economic situation; investments are made also when a large portion of capital assets is underutilised for lack of manpower and raw materials.

g) Agriculture

Agriculture has affirmed its position in the economy; 1985 again brought good crops and the crops continue to be satisfactory with yields of the four grain crops (wheat, barley, rye and oats) at over 30 quintals per hectare and that of rape 10% greater than the 1985 record. Yields in livestock farming have risen as well. In 1980 each million pigs yielded 142 thousand tons of animals for slaughter, while in 1985 the tonnage reached 157 thousand, or 10% more. In the first six months of 1986, the delivery of cattle for slaughter was still growing, to reach 200 thousand tons in July, an annual rate approaching the highest level since 1980. This performance is reflected on the market. The 'experimental' off-the-ration sale of privately slaughtered meat, introduced in February 1986, is being extended. From the point of view of economic rationality, the system is an oddity (only the producer has the right to sell, only the consumer to buy, and the transaction can only be made in the producer's voivodship, or province), but despite this, the private enterprise of producer/salesman is overcoming the obstacles and free market meat sales have spread throughout the country. Still, the rationing system remains and it has been suggested that it will be another five years before it can be abolished. It is more and more obviously economic nonsense, retained only for certain social – and perhaps political – reasons. The social reasons are the resentment and fear of a meat price rise to a level at which the present effective demand – i.e. the amount of money people are ready to spend on meat – would equal the present supply. The prices of privately slaughtered meat suggest that this rise could be kept to an average of 25%. But that is an average, and price differentiation, especially of smoked meats, should be considerably greater than it is now. Meanwhile, the 8% meat price rise in 1986 preserved the present structure of prices and made no progress towards a balance between different kinds of meat. From this point of view, then, this rise was a wasted opportunity. The reason was the authorities' fear of the people's reaction to too high prices of some kinds of meat.

In part I we mentioned that agriculture's recent good results had led to the hope that it might become an engine which could pull the economy out of the crisis and replace non-renewable raw material exports with renewable ones. We expressed our scepticism about this hope and we have not changed our view. The longer agriculture manages to perform well, the clearer it is that it will not become an engine for the economy. In the present economic system and with the huge shortages of capacity in the complementary links of manufacturing and trade, increased agricultural produce simply cannot be converted into an improvement in the whole of the economy, better industrial efficiency, a more balanced market, increased purchasing power for the zloty, and a better foreign trade balance. The outstanding crops of rape, for example, cause problems with its utilisation: obsolete oil mills are not able to process it and despite the abundance of the oil-bearing material there is a shortage of margarine on the market. Tomatoes produced a rich crop in 1986 too, but vegetable processing plants could not cope with all the fruit and there were no cans in which to pack the concentrated paste, because there is no suitable thin sheet metal, which would have to be bought abroad, as Poland's giant rolling mills are designed to make only thick armour plate.

Paradoxically, then, agriculture's good output is having an unfavourable impact on our economy: by creating a temporary abundance, by pacifying the food market, it produces an impression of overall economic improvement, an impression which is false. It is an illusion to which rulers and people alike succumb, an illusion that brings self-reassurance and the feeling that, in an important respect, the crisis has been overcome. Actually, nothing of the kind has happened, none of the central problems has been solved in the Polish economy, no causes that led to the crisis have been eradicated. The shelter offered by the more abundant food supply encourages the authorities to wait until the crisis wears off, making few, if any, changes in the system.

Why then is farming doing better than it used to and better than most of the economy? It is because agriculture as it is in Poland is a relatively autonomous segment of the economy and can function when only weakly connected with the rest of the economic system. It uses few industrially made means of production, and its output consists of staple commodities with low income elasticity of demand and a low degree of processing. Weather conditions and the toil of the private, individual farmer are both independent of the system. This being so, it was enough to apply a slightly less discriminatory policy toward this sector of the economy to see the results appear. But it will not be so forever. If agriculture is to develop it has to lose its autonomous character. It has to receive more inputs from industry, and its produce has to have a greater influence on the rest of the economy. The fact that yields of the four grains have not exceeded 30 quintals per hectare for a third year running suggests stagnation has already set in. In these conditions, this engine will not move any faster.

h) Exports to the West

In part I we pointed to the difficulties in foreign trade with capitalist countries which arose in the first half of 1985. This is the key portion of our trade. In the event, Poland's trade surplus with the West for the year was $1.1 billion, compared with a planned surplus of 1.5 billion. Since May 1986 exports to the West have been decreasing compared with the same time in 1985, by 15% in May, 11% in June, and as much as 20% in July. For the first six months taken together the fall was 3%. This inevitably affected imports from the West, which in May were down 4%, in June 8%, and July over 9%. This must have had an impact on supplies for current production, and might have been one of the reasons for the decline of output in May and June and the scant growth in July 1986.

Despite great efforts to switch the economy to closer cooperation with the Comecon countries and especially with the Soviet Union, the economic links with the West established in the 1970s are maintained and every boost in output must be preceded by a rise in imports from and followed by higher exports to the capitalist countries. Any difficulties in this trade bode ill for production. We have already mentioned the case of tomato paste which cannot be packed for want of tin cans. It can also be seen in broader phenomena: the Ministry of Foreign Trade no longer honours one of the few concrete benefits of the reform – the hard currency retention quota. The accounts still formally exist, and exporting companies earn interest on them, but the accounts have been frozen. All hard-currency earnings are once again at the central authorities' disposal.

The collapse of exports to the West brought a greatly shrunken surplus of $420 million for the first half of 1986, though the annual plan anticipated the same figure as in 1985 – $1.5 billion. Why has this happened? Official communiques offer no comment but certain things can be deduced. Stevedoring in commercial parts between January and July 1986 dropped 5.4% below the level for the same months of 1985, and in July itself the drop was 21%. This is accounted for by decreased shipments of coal, which again turns out to be the reason behind the decline

69

in the basic economic indices. The gap created by reduced coal exports could not be filled with industrial exports, which earn little hard currency.

Against this background, some comment is required on the reports of success supposedly achieved by the engineering industry in the form of greater exports to hard-currency markets. It is even thought of as no less than a breakthrough, a turning point in recent trends, for since the crisis began the industry's exports have been falling. And now, all of a sudden, the share has grown. But closer analysis shows that this is a rather peculiar achievement, and a transitory one, too. A large shipment of Polish cars was consigned to China, and since China settles the account in Swiss francs, it is treated as a hard-currency market. However, no durable development of exports can be based on a single deal. The Chinese car market cannot be expected to make the motor industry a modern equivalent of the 19th century textile industry of the Kingdom of Poland, nor can we hope that the industry's profits on this market will finance the reconstruction it urgently needs.

The weakness of hard-currency exports and the diminished trade surplus are the most serious symptoms of the crisis in which the economy is still stuck. Exports to Western markets are an objective test of our country's economic as well as organisational efficiency. Facing competitive hard-currency markets reveals all the economic weaknesses of the system; they cannot be covered up by propaganda, arbitrary edicts or monopolist dictates. And the mediocre financial performance of our exports must have an impact on Poland's position in the talks about our debt and, more important, about possible new credits. Debts already owed will be put off till later, new interest will be added, but with our hard-currency earnings tumbling, no new credits will be extended, and our membership of the IMF will not help.

2. Impoverishment and Declining Standard of Living

a) Real Wages

Having surveyed the production side of the economic process, we now turn our attention to its results in the form of consumption. People in Poland have become poorer as a result of the crisis. The shock it created was all the more painful since during the Gierek period real incomes, standard of living, and level of social consumption rose markedly. Gierek's socialism was not a socialism with a human face, but it was to be one with a satiated face. As we have noted, it was a false well-being since it had been obtained for borrowed money. In the late 1970s things started to go wrong, but *Solidarity* managed to prolong and even strengthen Gierek's pay and price policies for as long as it was active, although in real terms the economy, deprived of foreign credits and sabotaged by the authorities, was no longer able to produce the goods corresponding to the incomes won by *Solidarity*. Inflation ensued, at first mainly queue inflation, reflecting the huge imbalance on the market. The steep price rises put into effect in February 1982, under martial law, were supposed to restore balance by transforming the queue inflation into overt price inflation. As we know, this goal was not fully achieved though the market imbalance was reduced a little, but the operation revealed a drop in incomes and real wages in statistical, financial terms. The officially admitted drop was 25%. For the next two years wages remained unchanged, and in 1985 they rose slightly – by 3.6%. In the first half of 1986 nominal wages and other incomes probably kept slightly ahead of prices, just as they did in 1985.

b)Consumption

How, then, did people live in Poland in mid-1986 and how much poorer had they become after six years of economic crisis? The question cannot be answered in a single sentence for standards of living and degrees of impoverishment are varied, especially in a crisis. Besides, the term 'impoverishment' is vague and we feel that it cannot be confined to reduced real wages alone.

Let us see first what the effect on the structure of consumption has been. In 1980 the Polish population spent 31% of its total consumer budget on food; in 1984 the figure was 33%. In accordance with Engel's law, an increasing proportion of expenditure on food is a result of decreasing income. Yet, if we believe these figures, the change in the structure of consumption is small. Impoverishment looks somewhat worse when we examine consumption in physical units. The per capita consumption of meat (compared with the 1978-80 high mark) was 18% down in 1985, fruit 31% down, eggs 5% down, cotton fabric 15% down, and washing and cleaning agents 16% down. At the same time, the structure of food consumption continued to change in favour of higher value foods: grain products were 71% down and potatoes as much as 14% down.

The degree of impoverishment varied between different categories of consumer. Taking 1980 = 100, the nominal pay index in 1985 was 331 and the cost of living index 409. But the cost of food grew almost four and a half times, including fish – six times, alcohol five times, clothing three times, transport less than three and a half times, fuel and energy less than three times, home furnishings and services almost six times, postal services three and a half times. Thus *some* commodities were actually cheaper relative to wages in late 1985 than in 1980.

c) Social Impoverishment

We feel, however, that these statistics do not provide an exhaustive description. What help is it that the price of clothing grew less than nominal wages, if this clothing, and especially underwear, cannot be bought, just like hundreds of other items? For the quoted indexes are based on prices which are not equilibrium prices. In this respect the 1980s have brought a perceptible, sometimes even profound impoverishment or reduction in the standard of living.

1) The Collapse of the Market

The market for goods and services has suffered far-reaching disruption. This is not just a question of non-equilibrium prices. All aspects of the market are malfunctioning. Buying anything is always a dismal business, often a nightmare; it creates not only frustration but permanent stress as well. And where it concerns staple and essential commodities it also constitutes a permanent lowering of the quality of life and is a concrete form of impoverishment as it deprives people of the minimum comfort and security they are entitled to in a civilised world. No statistical indices of real wages show the depressing drabness and poverty of what is offered for sale. The food market is said to be in equilibrium, agriculture has been doing well for the past few years, but tens of thousands of grocery shops in cities and villages present such a poor range of products displayed in so primitively furnished a space that it is simply unbelievable that this is late twentieth-century Europe. Only some big stores in major cities give the impression of a certain variety. But this is not the case with stores selling manufactured goods. It has been like this for years and one may wonder what the connection is between stagnant coal production, or the slump in exports to the West, and the lack of the simplest sweets, or irregular supplies of bread.

This poverty of market supply makes the marginal utility of money low. Once the consumer has crossed an income threshold of around 20,-000 – 30,000 zlotys a month, which is required for current needs, there is nothing to spend extra money on until he crosses the next threshold of about 100,000 zlotys, for which some durable goods can be purchased. Another threshold is 1,000,000 zlotys, which makes it possible to buy a car or flat. Between these points there are dead ranges in which the marginal utility of money is low, which discourages improving work efficiency and helps to increase alcohol consumption, since alcohol is the only commodity which has a high income elasticity of demand and is available for all budget ranges. The rapid decline in the marginal utility of income is also due to the limited opportunities of investing savings as capital.

2) Housing

Nor does the real-wage index embrace certain important fields which, as products and services, help to meet the population's needs. The most significant are housing and medical care.

The drop in the construction of flats from 280,000 in 1978 to 190,-000 per year in the 1980s has increased the waiting tme for a flat to more than twelve years and lowered the standard of living of hundreds of thousands of people. Stagnant or, in the major cities, falling construction rates have become a permanent element of the Polish economy of the 1980s. The government pursues a double-faced policy. On the one hand, it makes declarations on the social importance of housing, on the necessity to boost construction (to 400,000 flats annually) and even set up a special Housing Council, but on the other, cuts the production and supplies of building materials, impedes the allocation of sites, delays the provision of services for sites, and then announces that construction should actually be slowed down so as to reduce future energy demand. It has been calculated that a million new flats require an additional 1,000 megawatts; with people sharing flats more often as the population grows more numerous, power consumption is increased only slightly.

3) Health Care

Universal medical care provided by the state was to have been a great achievement of socialism, and at first it looked as if this would be accomplished. Extending social security to rural areas in the 1970s made it truly universal. Unfortunately, this vast and ambitious project was inadequately supported with personnel, equipment, and facilities. Since the 1960s, in fact, the quality of the service has been worsening, especially in out-patient treatment. Now the state medical service is, at best, stagnating, which renders it incapable of meeting growing needs, and in some respects the stagnation must be called a decline. It is particularly conspicuous in three aspects: staff, hospital beds and medicines.

For many years now, the health service has been increasingly suffering from a shortage of staff, both doctors, particularly specialist, and middle and lower level hospital staff. Statistically, there are fewer doctors in Poland per head of population than the European average, but in practice the deficit is much more severe than the figures indicate. Out-patient care is the area worst affected by the shortage of doctors. An appointment with a specialist requires weeks of waiting, and in branches like ophthalmology, weeks become months. There are not nearly enough dentists and dental technicians. It is almost impossible to get a slightly non-standard denture made by the state health service. The shortage of nurses is even more acute, especially in hospitals. Great difficulties are also caused in hospitals by insufficient numbers of ward attendants. This places great strain on patients, as well as not allowing even a bare minimum of cleanliness to be maintained.

The shortage of personnel in the health service results partly from inefficient work organisation and the overburdening of doctors with bureaucratic procedures, but also from insufficient medical training and education facilities. A decade ago limits were imposed on enrolment for dental studies and the outcome now is a scarcity of dentists.

The reason for the shortage of middle and lower personnel is low pay. There are too few nurses and attendants because not many are willing to do these jobs, which are difficult, often responsible, and invariably underpaid. Low pay afflicts all of the medical service. Doctors earn less than workmen; a newly qualified doctor's earnings are close to the poverty level (in late 1985 – 9,000 zlotys a month) while a worker his age makes twice as much. But a doctor's choice of profession is motivated in part by a moral factor: satisfaction, self-fulfilment, intellectual curiosity. This is less true of nurses and attendants, so the shortage of these categories is worst. Insufficient personnel and low pay have caused a decline in the standard of medical care. This is conspicuous in the work of doctors, whose actions are not confined to routine. Superimposed on this is the national medical system's organisational inefficiency, which also reduces public confidence in the medical service. As a result some patients choose to go to medical cooperatives or private practitioners. Yet the growth of doctors' cooperatives has been obstructed for years, and private practices are limited by a lack of suitable accommodation as well as by the smaller and smaller number of doctors who have adequate professional training to undertake private practice.

Out-patient care is the first stage of a patient's contact with the national health service; the second is hospital with its shortage of beds. In Poland, the number of hospital beds per 10,000 inhabitants is among the lowest in Europe (only Greece, Yugoslavia and Portugal have less) and since 1980 the figure has been going down. An average hospital takes more than ten years to build, some hospitals are closed and undergoing lengthy repairs, equipment often fails, laboratories work at a sluggish rate. Consequently, hospital beds are under great pressure; the wait for a bed is weeks or months; emergency beds in hospital corridors are commonplace. Despite this, owing to poor organisation, patients are made to stay in hospital for prolonged periods of time, aggravating the scarcity.

The third problem is medicines. The supply of drugs, small medical apparatus, and dressing materials has been insufficient for years, but in the 1980s it became disastrous. This is not merely a figure of speech, as for someone who has to take medicines such as psychotropic drugs all the time a sudden lack of them is a real disaster. For a time there were no painkillers; now cardiac drugs are scarce; adhesive bandages have been unavailable for quite a time now; basic anti-cold remedies periodically disappear all of a sudden. Not only imported medicines are scarce, but also those manufactured domestically, as well as herbal preparations. Disposable syringes and needles are in short supply, which makes every injection a risk of contracting a contagious disease (most often a viral inflammation of the liver).

Medicines are cheap in Poland; the insured pay 30% of the price, pensioners get them free of charge. But persistent shortages of even the most rudimentary drugs undermine the advantages of this nationalised distribution, create uncertainty and fear (sometimes well justified), and force people to go about trying to obtain foreign drugs and preparations either as aid from abroad (received in quantity by hospitals) or as expensive purchases (given the dollar's black market rate of exchange).

The deteriorating standard of health care as well as the degeneration of the environment have begun to affect the population's health.

This is shown by the reduction in life expectancy. It is especially true for men and has even acquired a name of its own: male hypermortality. During the last ten years the life expectancy of a forty-five year old man dropped (according to official statistics) from 27.5 to 26.5 years, or by 3.6%).

4) Natural Environment

The real wage statistics omit yet another factor which has significant importance for the quality of life, namely the state of the natural environment. In part I we discussed the environment as a barrier to industrial and agricultural production. Now it is time to consider the environment's consumer aspect. Clean water, clean air, unpolluted soil are needed, not only for production, but first of all for survival. But they are ever harder to find in Poland. The most important is water. In some areas it is severely polluted, or simply not there. We shall not repeat the basic statistics on precipitation rates and total water consumption, or the degrees of pollution of rivers. Let us look at the problem from the point of view of a consumer of water. In big cities it is not fit for drinking without intense boiling, and even then it reeks of chlorine. In Warsaw the water must be specially filtered to make good tea. But the problem is not only taste. This contaminated water carries some chemical compounds which cause stomach and kidney diseases. In some areas soil dehydration following mining means that water has to be piped from remote reservoirs, which are only half-built. The situation is worst in Silesia and in the Bielsko-Biala region. Whole neighbourhoods of blocks of flats have been built which have no water; villas have bathrooms elegantly tiled, with taps from which no water has ever flowed. Such a severe shortage of water causes a health danger from unpurified sewage which is drained into the nearest river or creek; waste in leaking, unemptied cesspools gives off a stench. This is accompanied by a dangerous phenomenon: people are getting used to it, do not take precautions, do not even express indignation.

It is no better with air. Travelling across the country by train or by car, all of a sudden we have to close the windows as we enter a zone of putrid industrial air. Silesia's air is polluted with sulphur dioxide from industry, and in Warsaw it is no better, because of exhaust fumes. In tree-lined streets we can see spots where trees are withering and dying. The spots are bus stops, where the exhaust of buses kills plants. It kills people too, only more slowly.

Air pollution threatens large areas of coniferous forests. For example, the whole population of spruce in the Karkonosze mountains is already dying out. Elsewhere, lowered water tables are killing deciduous forests too. Bad water and bad air also threaten spas, half of which are already surrounded with industry and urban processes and are effectively ceasing to be health resorts.

Reversing or merely halting the process of water, air, and soil degeneration requires immense capital expenditure. Plans have resolved that in the coming years the priority will be given to water investment projects: reservoirs, pipelines, sewage treatment plants. But can people wait?

5) Infrastructure

Progressive deterioration is affecting the whole of the cities' technical infrastructure: houses, streets, parks, underground heat lines, sewers, waterworks. What is out of sight is out of mind – until a failure occurs. But what can be seen is conspicuous and felt; the state of streets and especially of pavements in cities is lamentable, not only for lack of maintenance, but also for the low quality of cement used in the manufacture of slabs, which seems to lack any binding properties. Severe deterioration has also occurred in the railway infrastructure: track, rolling stock, stations and other buildings present a picture of decline. All these are aspects of the population's impoverishment too.

6) Production Quality

Another area of impoverishment is the quality of production and services. Suddenly everything has got worse. Inferior quality plagues not only technologically sophisticated products, but also simple ones, made for tens or hundreds of years. So we have cement that does not bind because dust is added to it, milk that goes sour right away, eggs that have no yolks, towels that do not dry (artificial fibres), brooms that do not sweep (artificial bristles) and thinner and thinner fabrics.

The above survey of phenomena that could be termed non-income pauperisation of the population indicates that pauperisation – like many other things – has a different dimension in socialism than in capitalism. In socialism, the impoverishment – apart from being visible in falling real incomes and in family budgets has an added social dimension and this, though for the time being not as acutely felt, is perhaps more important. For there is no escaping the social aspect of pauperisation, the impoverishment of the country. Lower and higher income groups alike must endure the hardships of the socialist way of life: breathe polluted air, drink contaminated water, stand in queues, purchase meat and petrol with rationing coupons, buy shoddy products, shiver with cold in their flats because of a heating failure, run about the town looking for medicines, be treated in overcrowded and ill-functioning hospitals.

d) Stratification – Poverty and Affluence

Only two things can give partial shelter from the results of social pauperisation: power and big money. Therefore, two groups of people are, to a degree, immune to this process. Those in power enjoy concrete privileges which shield them from the impoverishment spreading all over the country: they have separate shops and special allocations of goods, separate neighbourhoods and comfortable houses (though the comfort is of a meagre, socialist kind), their own hospitals, sanatoria, and resorts.

But they must still breathe the same polluted air, drink the same water, and even eat some foods of the same inferior quality (although Gierek, for example, had his and his family's milk imported from Holland).

Big money can also provide relief from some of socialism's distinctive features, but it is not as effective as privilege. But neither can free people from the kind of impoverishment which is caused by the tedium of socialism.

The rest of society is fully subjected to social pauperisation regardless of their earnings and family budgets. To be sure, amid this general indigence, some fare better than others. Workers skilled in essential professions employed in big factories, in private businesses, or the six hundred small foreign firms operating in Poland earn high nominal sums and their real wages today are even higher than at the peak of the Gierek boom. However, in order to put the matter in perspective, these earnings in zlotys should be converted into real money. The official rate of exchange is $1 to 200 zlotys. This is close enough to the relative purchasing power of the two currencies. At this exchange rate a high hourly rate of pay is $1, an average monthly pay $120, miners' pay $300 a month. And even at such low rates the money cannot be fully spent on goods.

Compared with a large proportion of workers, individual farmers obtain higher earnings if they manage their land well. Workers and farmers are people of hard physical toil that must be appreciated. They are privileged as regards pay, but the product of their work is not an idea, a technical, organisational, or economic improvement, not cultural values. They alone will not get the country out of the mire.

We must also consider the so-called second economy. A large section of the labour force in Poland takes up additional, unofficial (sometimes even illegal) work and these people generate a concrete, 'primary' product, in no way inferior to that generated by miners or metal workers, though ignored by the official statistics. This work provides goods and services to be bought with some of the money issued by the state, thus alleviating inflation, and brings those that generate it a certain affluence. This partly accounts for quite lively growth of private construction jobs in Poland. For the private sector and the second economy the characteristically socialist expansion of demand constitutes an automatic stimulus.

Below the pay levels of workers and individual farmers are the masses of 'unproductive sphere' employees, from clerks to teachers, doctors, actors, writers and academics. They all constitute the proletariat in modern Poland: if they do not eke out their income, they live modestly and suffer as well as social impoverishment. The low salaries of this group – which includes even engineers – prove that socialism does not create a need for work of a higher order, intellectyual, conceptual work. They feel superfluous as the usefulness of their work is limited and unclear in this system, while the work of a shovel-swinging workman or a bus driver is concrete and brings visible utility.

The relationship between the incomes of these two social groups proves that Poland has been affected by so-called decomposition of the components of the social status of individual groups within the population: income level does not correspond to social status, education, culture and position in the social division of labour. Consequently, culturally higher social groups lose their standard-setting position and cease to be seen by the rest of the society as worthy of emulation in customs and values. Even cultural snobbery, which used to propagate these values at least outwardly, is vanishing too. This is another sign of society's impoverishment, a curious manifestation of Engel's law, and it is directly reflected in the pattern of consumption. People obtaining higher income, but deprived of cultural background, have a poor consumption pattern. Add to this young people's lack of a flat of their own, or one of sufficient size, and the consequence is a further impoverishment of the structure of consumption since most durable goods occupy square footage. Consequently, in the workmen's and farmers' consumption pattern more and more prominence is given to alcohol,, to which the population devotes over 12% of its total expenditure. From the point of view of the people's state, which is responsible for delivering goods to be bought with the money it issues, this is a very effective kind of commodity. With a different social distribution of spending, they would have to supply the market with more goods and services that would be less profitable than vodka.

Pensioners are even lower than the white collar proletarians, and are followed by the near-bottom level of families afflicted with social or individual health problems. But the pauperisation of the population should not be viewed only from the angle of these, basically marginal, social groups, nor should our attention concentrate solely on the poor. There are poor people everywhere, in America as well as Poland. But in Poland the whole of society has been made socially poor. The pauperisation of a country is not expressed in a million families' living below poverty leve, but in the absence of any really rich people and of an affluent middle class on a socially significant scale; the existing 'steeples' of income and privilege have an uncertain social position and are by no means free from the consequences of social pauperisation.

3. Prognoses Verified

It is time to start formulating certain forecasts for the immediate future. During the year which has passed since the analysis in parts I and II were written, all our predictions regarding technical issues proved true. There was indeed a price rise for a number of goods and services, from food to transport, though the program was not fully accomplished. Vodka and cigarette prices will be increased a second time, since the first one passed imperceptibly. There were two consecutive devaluations of the zloty against the dollar, and the rouble. Foreign trade with the West went as predicted. Our forecast regarding progress of the reform came true too: there was no progress; systemic issues and principles of regulation were frozen in a trasitional stage and this 'reserve' was not utilised.

However, the pay policy which we predicted the authorities would implement was not adopted. Instead of halting the stress of pay rises, which seemed intolerable, when contrasted with stagnant production, they simply prolonged the situation which according to rational calculation, they should have tackled last year. They gave up trying to reach, or even approach, equililbrium, which in the opinion of all economists is the basic and necessary requilrement for the functioning of the economic reform's principles, in overcoming stagnation and paralysis, and achieving a breakthrough in efficiency. Instead, they decided consciously to maintain the policy of adding fuel to the overt and latent inflation by uncontrolled growth of wages and other incomes, against which the price increases planned and introduced proved no match. Why did they do it and why were they able to? Essentially, they repeated Gierek's manoeuvre of buying people off, particularly the working class of big factories, paying them more despite the absence of more goods and services. They did it because any policy of halting or blocking wages – which, by the way, is continually announced in the press and in government declarations –threatens a confrontation with the working masses. Under the present political circumstances, such a cure for the economy cannot be administered without a tug of war that the Jaruzelski government, entangled in the programme of normalisation, cannot afford now. Therefore, the prediction of the scenario sketched in part II could be treated as a warning.

How could the authorities continue this wage policy without a further, disastrous aggravation of economic equililbrium? Two factors can be identified which made it possilble. The first is agriculture and the food market. Part of the riising stream of income was channelled into food and the impact absorbed by the food market. The decisive part was played by meat, which found its way to the market, by-passing the rationing system, and absorbed some of the additional income. The importance of the food market in this respect is illustrated by the sales growth index. From January to July, retail food sales climbed by 26.5%, while the sales of non-food goods rose only 20%.

But of course, the income elasticity of demand for food is limited and the food market could not absorb all of the population's income increase. The rest – after spending on non-food commodities and services, whose supply grew negligibly or not at all – had to be saved, in the form of increased financial resources, i.e. in the inflationary overhang. They are then, typical empty zlotys. Why do people work for empty zlotys and, in particular, why do peasants do so and accumulate heaps of money, since they have less opportunity to exchange it for goods than townspeople? Another circmstance plays a role here, and it plays into the government's hands: people are financial nominalists and this psychological property helps the authorities in any inflation. As long as the currency depreciates at less than a gallop, as long as money can buy something, even with a bribery surcharge, people will accept money and are ready to exchange their work for it. This is why the authorities managed to prolong the inflationary flow of currency by another year.

4. The Second Stage of the Reform

It should nevertheless be stressed that from the angle of the economy's interests, this policy is harmful since it delays any possible solution that would halt the process of degradation of the market, the currency, and the entire economy. It is, furthermore, a policy that does not solve anything, as the reasons necessitating the strict income-curbing measures we anticipated have not been removed. The economy, the manufacturing machine, proved unable to respond to increased financial demand with an appropriately higher and suitably structured supply. Everything is the way it used to be, only worse the longer it lasts. So we repeat: the question is not if the authorities will undertake measures to limit the people's demand, chiefly by freezing wages, the question is when will they try to do it. At the time of writing, in the third quarter of 1986, they have less time than they did a year ago. But we cannot rule out the possibility that they will again try to postpone the moment of truth.

a) Preparing a New Wage Policy

Government propaganda is more and more often heralding the introduction of a restrictive wage policy. But since the issue is extremely difficult and carries great political risk, the authorities wish to invoke the highest formal authority they can create, namely the party congress. For the past few months, then, there have been constant repetitions that the 10th Congress voted this or that and now whatever is done is and will be in implementation of the Congress' decisions. And what did the Congress decide in economic matters? It resolved that the condition for fulfilling the goals set in the National Social-Economic Plan for 1986-1990 was 'definite progress in achieving equililbrium in the economy, and this requires first of all passing on to the second stage of the economic reform'. We had not previously heard about the division of the reform into stages, incidentally, but now all of a sudden the second stage pops up in a situation in which it is clear for everyone that no first stage has been completed yet.

Presenting the attack on the population's standard of living as a necessity stemming from the economic reform is a clever move for it foils the criticism from those who were in favour of consistent enforcement of the reform, and thus also criticism by the political opposition.

What then is the second stage about? 'It should ensure the introduction and operation of an economic mechanism compelling economic agents to intensify actions aimed at improving the efficiency of the economy.' Furthermore, it is supposed to bring inflation down to a single-digit level by 1990, provided there is 'a firm and consistent policy in shaping incomes and prices'. (Quotations from a PAP report on a Planning Commission session.) In other words, in the language of typical bureaucratic proclamations, measures such as we sketched last year are announced. The propaganda campaign we mentioned in the scenario even began in early September 1986. According to a Politbureau communique, 'this campaign will enable us to determine the rate at which to introduce stricter requirements of efficiency in companies'. It is to 'prepare the work force and cultivate social readiness to accept these resolutions'. High level functionaries went round visiting big factories and talking to the workers. One can expect their consultations to be followed by some concrete instructions on implementing the economic compulsion of which the Planning Commission report spoke.

Another pointer in the same direction is the so-called 'job attestation' throughout the state and cooperative economy, as well as in the directly state-financed sphere, and an associated review of organisational structures. The vague way of describing this (which was also voted by the 10th Congress) suggests that its main point is to cut employment and to obtain some labour reserve.

Taking all these actions now and in such a sweeping way indicates that the authorities are aware of the actual economic situation and of the impossibility of maintaining the present economic policy. The questions that have to be asked here are: are they fully aware of it? And will they be able to carry out this new policy? In other words, will it work?

What exactly is this economic compulsion to produce and whom is it supposed to affect? It is to embrace companies and their work force. This new slogan contains nothing that is not known from previous statements on the reform. The point is actually to introduce strict self-financing under which companies must meet their costs out of their own revenues. If this is done it will create an automatic link between wages and market-verified production results, which means that wage inflation will cease and thus the present uncontrolled growth of incomes will be curbed. The whole operation is to be explained as the effect of objective and impersonal economic forces, of economic necessity. The authorities will claim that they are not responsible for it, and it is no use addressing wage claims to them. Their primary and basic motive in declaring the reform, in fact, was and is the desire to pass the responsibility for wages (and prices) on to companies and their management and then to the objective conditions and results of their work. The scheme is well advanced and an instruction has been prepared on 'new principles of regulating the inflow of funds for wages in the productive sphere'.

b) What else is Economic Compulsion supposed to do?

Of course, economic compulsion is not supposed just to settle the question of wages. Its tasks are broader than that for it is to be the main agent eliciting economic efficiency from companies. In this sense, economic compulsion as a force leading to greater efficiency in the entire national economy is a concept approximating Adam Smith's famous 'invisible hand'. As we haave already said, the concept of economic compulsion is consistent with the logic of the proclaimed reform and constitutes a development of the principle of company self-financing. How then should we evaluate these intentions and their chances of realisation? Will the reform succeed?

It is quite improbable that the communists should manage to introduce objective economic compulsion fully and consistently into the economy (and it is only on such a scale that it can bring the expected results) and be able and willing to bear all the economic, and particularly the political, costs involved. If economic compulsion is to cure the economy, it cannot be confined to companies and their work force, but should encompass the state and its organs too. In market economies the state is subjected to economic compulsion and can carry out interventionist policies only within narrow boundaries. But a totalitarian communist state, the owner of most of the capital goods, the sole author and supervisor of the central economic plan, cannot by itself yield to objective economic compulsion since it would destroy its identity. On the contrary, it does its best to institute coercion for all its economic agents while itself remaining beyond its scope. Thus it is by no means economic compulsion, but political and administrative coercion, not impersonal but exercised by a concrete, personified political system. It is not an invisible hand – it is a hand that can be clearly seen and its owner identified. The peculiarity of this coercion is evident in the attempts to lay down new wage regulations. They prescribed various formulae determining tax-free wage limits, taking into account the varied operating conditions of individual industries. It is supposed to be a departure from arbitrariness, but obviously it is still arbitrariness, only codified. For who determined the differentiation? The authorities, of course; an unambiguously visible hand. The weakness underlying such 'economic' compulsion consists in the fact that behind all this rigour, these commands and conditions, one can always see a definite person, office or institution, and thus this compulsion becomes subjective and relative. From here, it is a short step to efforts to relax limits and by-pass orders by claiming actual objective difficulties. Decades of experience of annual plan revision in the last month of the year prove that all this is not real economic compulsion but an economic game. The same thing is manifest now when an attempt is made, in accordance with the reform, to declare a company insolvent. So far, none has gone bankrupt, despite fully deserving to, as some sponsor will always turn up (usually the 'founding organ', i.e. the superior ministry or local authority), obtain money from the state treasury, and bail the bankrupt firm out. What is worse, everybody knows beforehand that this will happen. This ultimate responsibility of the state for every company is logically justified: the conditions in which individual economic agents – companies – function are largely created by the state. Prices of products, of capital goods, supply restrictions and allocations, and finally the basic structure of output – all these are imposed on a company, which has no freedom to choose more profitable parameters. It is therefore impossible to determine what portion of the loss is due to the company's own inefficiency, and what results from conditions forced upon it.

Let us give a concrete example of the subjectivity of the economic compulsion now operating. Demand for cement in Poland far exceeds supply. As a result, the black-market price reaches 20,00 zlotys a ton, or nearly one month's average pay. But the official price is a fraction of that, and this is the price which the producer receives. In this situation, some cement plants incur huge losses and are facing bankruptcy. The reason? They do not receive adequate coal or fuel oil and in consequence suffer prolonged shutdowns while their fixed costs (including wages, as their work force cannot be dismissed) have to be met. But does this show that such a plant has not managed to measure up to the requirements of economic compulsion and should be closed down? Obviously not. The solution that would be provided by a truly economic and truly objective compulsion is this: The prices of cement and fuel would increase to an equilibrium level, fuel rationing would be abandoned, and employment would be made flexible. A plant which would not cover the high costs of fuel out of its revenue from higher-priced cement would go bankrupt. Under competition, those plants which could do so, that is to say, the most efficient ones, would remain, while cement would go to those buyers who could pay the new, higher price – again the most efficient users.

Therefore economic compulsion, if it is to exert a correcting influence on the economic process and enforce efficiency, should be, first, fully objective, i.e. result from independent action of a multitude of economic agents, which is only ensured by the market. Second, economic agents must have the freedom to choose, for only then can they be expected, when faced with objective (market) parameters, to make the best of their situation.

c) The Socialist Version of Economic Compulsion

But let us assume that the authorities who so often quote the decisions of the 10th party Congress attempt to go deeper into the recommendations of the economic reform and treat economic compulsion seriously. Certain circumstances indicate that such an intention may be entertained; what would happen then? The new policy would begin 'from within'. This means that the authorities would impose economic compulsion on companies and their work force with unchanged prices and continued rationing of capital goods. Numerous companies now functioning thanks to individual tax reductions would then run into severe losses and have to be closed down. Some plants would be taken over by other factories, but for most it would be physical liquidation – perhaps even removing their machines and abandoning their buildings. The work force would be dismissed, some skilled employees would quickly find jobs in neighbouring companies, and the management would also be given new posts, but most workers would find themselves unemployed, at least initially. This would relieve the tension on the labour market, but then the negative consequences of local unemployment would come to the fore.

The closure of a company would affect its suppliers and customers. The suppliers would have lost some of their market, which could disrupt their production and organisation, necessitating a switch to another line of production, cutting employment, changing sub-contractors and making additional investments. Customers will be hurt too: the company would have gone bankrupt not because it could not sell or made an unwanted product, but because, as a marginal producer, it could not keep its costs down within rigid prices. Its closure will cause a gap in production and shortages for its customers. If it produces an intermediate product, subsequent stages of manufacturing will be affected. As a result, the social production process will be disorganised, and sub-contracting arrangements disrupted. However, the efficiency of the whole economy will not improve. Why not? There are two reasons why this process, typical as it is for a capitalist, market economy, will prove disadvantageous in Poland. The first is that the judgement on the company condemning it to closure was based on a false calculation in which the principal parameters were unreal prices (cf. the above example of cement), which did not reflect the social demand for the company's product. Even if the factory closed had the highest costs in the industry, if its production was still needed to meet demand at a price which covered its costs, this factory should have remained in operation. The other reason is that in a free market economy, if a factory is closed down and a gap in supply is felt, other entrepreneurs will expand output or new ones enter the industry to fill the gap. But the pre-conditions for such action are a capital market and a surplus of production capacity. Under socialism, there is no capital market, no 'free entry', and by the time a 'founding organ' makes up its mind to form a new enterprise, negative results will already have damaged the economy.

The above argument shows that certain methods taken over from a capitalist economy and implanted in a socialist one with its artificial parameter structure and lack of flexibility can only bring losses. Trying to restructure the manufacturing machine and improve efficiency in this way, 'from within', is bound to fail. What this method might do is relieve the pressure on wages, and even somewhat increase work discipline in view of the threat of unemployment. In practice, however, this is hardly likely because the authorities will not go as far as we have indicated, even though they should. After the first, dramatic results, they will retreat, frightened, and confine themselves to verbal declarations on reform, restructuring and improving efficiency. The ostentatiously announced attestation of jobs and technologies, together with a verification of organisational structures, will fade away – it is clear even now – into petty make-believe actions. As far as organisational structures themselves are concerned, the powerful production monopolies would have to be broken up, and there is not enough determination for that.

Determination is also lacking in wage policy. It is therefore plausible to believe that in practice the authorities will not really be able to stop the rise of money wages. Though the task of achieving economic equilibrium is still a most urgent one, and given the supply-side rigidity, it cannot be achieved with the present rate of increase in nominal incomes, the dramatic scenario previously outlined in part II is not an imminent threat. Wages and incomes will keep climbing, people's savings will keep growing in face value and being reduced by two-thirds by inflation, companies will go on applying for subsidies and tax reductions, production will continue to rise and fall slightly, foreign debts will continue to be postponed for successive five-year periods, and interest on them will continue to be added to the principal outstanding. The motto of the current rulers is: No radical change, no about-face, keep the present 'normalisation' going as long as possible, maybe we can somehow survive this crisis (or rather decline) and remain in power.

d) Will There be a Currency Reform?

This political philosophy also precludes any radical moves in financial matters. In the aftermath of another devaluation of the zloty on 1 September 1986 rumours and fears of a currency reform reappeared. All rational premises combine to exclude such a possibility. Any currency reform is the result of some ailment of a country's economy. Healthy economies have had their currencies for tens or even hundreds of years. Still, not every currency reform is prompted by the same impulses or has the same goals. Three kinds can be distinguished. It can be a technical change which consists in lowering the face value of a currency by a factor of 100 or 1000. All the values expressed in money (prices, wages, taxes, etc.) are divided by 100 or 1000 and all relationships remain the same. A technical change of this kind is made when inflation has increased nominal values to such an extent that using them becomes inconvenient, e.g. limiting the use of calculating machines. This in fact is hardly a currency reform. A technical currency reform was recently carried out in Israel and one is planned in Italy.

The second type of change is an economic one and deserves the name of currency reform. It was executed not long ago in two Latin American countries: Brazil and Argentina. This kind includes the conversion of the mark into the zloty in Poland in 1923. Here, too, the reason was high inflation, but in this case the point was not just to lower the nominal values but primarily to quench the inflation and stabilise the currency. changing its name was an outward element of the reform intended to act psychologically to create trust in the new money.

Finally, the third kind is a predatory currency reform, such as took place in Poland in October 1950 and is still remembered (by a third generation now). The intent of such a measure, which is no reform either, is to take away part or all of the financial resources accumulated by the population in the form of savings or liquid assets.

At present, the conditions are not right for any of these types. A technical change is not going to be made as the cost of the operation would not be justified by consequent advantages. An economic change, or a currency reform proper, is not going to be undertaken as the authorities have no programme for stopping inflation, let alone achieving economic equilibrium. Without this, the curency would be no more stable and would immediately resume its depreciation, so the whole operation would prove useless.

Finally, a predatory reform is unlikely, too, although it would be the most attractive for the authorities. But today, unlike in 1950, there is simply no one to rob. Then the problem was clear: greater financial resources were in the possession of the survivors from the 'enemy classes' – the remaining bourgeoisie, rich peasants – and the predatory reform was both a tool and a stage in the class struggle: it was in fact expropriation. Besides the communists were on the offensive: they aimed to curb the role of money in the economy and believed that people's power, with the help of the central plan, could perform all economic functions. Today it is the reverse. They are conscious of their systemic defeat, are retreating (tactically!), and, to the accompaniment of declarations about reform, are seeking help in stimulating the economy from market forces and those social groups they once considered class enemies. They cannot, therefore, harm the liquid assets of that increasingly important economic sector and destroy the (minimal) trust of the social groups behind it. As far as non-productive financial resources are concerned, they are inviolable (excepting inflationary erosion), as a large portion of them belong to the people who are the authorities' political clients and any predatory reform would undercut their political base.

So there is not going to be a currency reform. Yet the zloty is not a currency to trust. Not only does it constantly lose value (some 20% a year), but, what is worse, the area of its usefulness is narrowing, while that of the dollar, which services an ever growing volume of goods, is broadening, in official as well as unofficial circulation. The chain of Pewex stores (in which goods can be bought only for hard currencies) is expanding, and major private transactions (buying and selling cars, flats, works of art) are increasingly made in dollars (of course illegally).

5. An Abstract Scenario for a Transition to a New System

The picture of the Polish economy emerging in late 1986 is even more grim than the one we drew in 1985. This is because this state of affairs has lasted a year longer, and so the destructive processes have progressed and the decline is deeper. In this situation, a natural question to ask is what, if anything, could be done to stop the process of decline and then reverse the course of events and propel the economy onto a new path of development? The need for this is voiced by the nation; the population is growing and needs a growing economy too.

There have been many programmes for overcoming the crisis and speeding up the economy. Recently, the communists have been doing nothing but making one plan after another to cure the declining economy. Some individual proposals in them are sound. That they do not produce the expected results proves that the root of the problem lies deeper. An economy is a system in which thousands of elements are intertwined and no single or partial action can change the system as a whole. To do this, systemic action has to be undertaken as well, i.e. regulating action encompassing the whole system, or specifically, all the main interrelationships between its individual elements and components. This implies that all aspects of such a systemic programme must be implemented simultaneously. Individual actions then combine to reinforce one another and the system begins to work. But given the size of the system that a national economy represents, it is impossible to carry out such a programme from one, central point. The programme of revitalising and boosting the economy must be split up and assigned to thousands of economic agents, whose action is directed and coordinated by a built-in economic homeostasis – the principle of economy.

The economic reform was to have been just such a systemic programme but its authors provided that it was to be carried out from a single centre, which would keep its central functions during and after the implementation of the reform. This was clear from the statements, repeated many times, that the reform aimed at strengthening central planning. Such a reform cannot be carried out; if the centre is to retain its functions the system must be declared unreformable.

Let us assume, however, that this oppressive centre disappears, though we keep a minimum of power to send signals through the decentralised programme of economic recovery. What would we need to do then? The imperative to implement all aspects simultaneously remains, but the particular areas in which the process will take place and phases it will go through need to be enumerated.

The first area on which to act is the market – the place where supply and demand meet. Free prices must be allowed immediately; they will oscillate around and settle fairly quickly at a level equating demand with supply at a given time. This is a fairly easy process, although in some areas a certain resistance may be encountered and price oscillation may be slower there.

The second field of action is companies. Production and supply monopolies must be broken up, industrial groups disbanded and all price arrangements abolished. Conditions for competition must be created and, most important, the principle of free entry to production and access to the market enforced. Inside companies entrepreneurs must be created out of employee self-management councils, i.e. they must be entrusted with the company and charged with full responsibility for its performance, including the bearing of risk. Companies must be given access to producers' goods at equilibrium prices, i.e. all allocation must be abolished. A capital market must be permitted to develop and foreign capital allowed access to existing enterprises and to create new ones.

The third area is households. Purchasing power (financial resources) in the possession of households at the moment the process begins must be maintained at its face value and confronted with free prices on the market. There is absolutely no reason to fear the overall level of prices rising high enough to threaten the population's subsistence. But relative prices will change substantially. What will independent trade unions do in these circumstances? Of course, they will struggle to secure better pay and working conditions for their members. But they will be facing not the state, but companies, and in former state-owned enterprises, their partners in negotiation will be representatives of employee self-management acting as employers. It will be a social benefit if these negotiations are treated seriously. In the new system wages will be settled by agreement between companies and trade unions.

The fourth area of change will be economic relations with other countries. Here, free buying and selling of foreign currencies by banks should be instituted, which will amount to convertibility of the zloty. The purchasing and selling price of a currency (its exchange rate) will be determined by supply and demand. Obviously, the dollar black market will collapse, which will be bad news for some. All companies must be allowed to do business with foreign partners.

The fifth area of systemic transformation should be the state budget, which should be reduced to administrative, social, and cultural issues. The subsidising of some companies out of taxes raised from other companies for this purpose should be ended. Companies should be left to raise wages to compensate for the increased prices of goods and services no longer subsidised.

State welfare programmes should be severed from the budget and transformed into funds separately financed and balanced. Local budgets should also be separated from the state budget, and local self-government bodies given their own income and independence in spending; transferring (taking over) local budget surpluses to the state budget should be discontinued. Big unfinished investment projects should be sold to the existing or newly-formed economic agents, even on credit. Investment projects in infrastructure should be carried on; their future utilisation should be based on economic calculation and charges levied where practicable.

Generally speaking, the state should retreat to its traditional domain: administration, civil service, but within this framework it should strengthen its controlling function over production and commerce from the angle of health (food), safety, and natural environment, and enforce strict compliance with standards in these fields. Finally, the state should operate special compensation funds (perhaps obtained from abroad) to alleviate the difficulties connected with rapid adjustment processes.

The sixth area of activity will be the functioning of money and the capital market. The functions of the central bank should be separated from the state budget; the issue of money and bank credit policy should be determined solely by economic requirements. The flow of money, both as capital and as consumption purchasing power, must stimulate real processes of production, trade and consumption and control the flow of goods and services. The structure of production and services must be adapted to match effective demand for consumption and capital goods. Capital would be available in the form of bank credit at a certain price – the interest rate, and other market forms of raising capital should also be allowed (stocks).

After these general changes have been implemented, adjustment movements would follow in companies, households, and the state budget sphere. Fairly quickly, these movements would bring about a new equilibrium in these three areas, but of course with profound changes in the structure of production and of consumption by households and the state budget. Companies subjected to the discipline of economic calculation, the requirements of self-financing, and pressure from competition would make their production suit the demand. These structural changes would lead to the elimination, or at least a radical reduction, of the idle sector, i.e. mainly the arms industry, its suppliers and contractors. The industry's factories would either switch to a different line of production, or find a way to export their existing output profitably.

The eliminating of the present excess demand would make selling goods more difficult. This would merely signify normalisation of the market and would be beneficial, since it would create competitive pressure on companies and be the surest way of improving the quality of production. After the adaptation movements have been completed, a new level of production and consumption will have been established, and from there, a new, balanced economic growth could begin.

The above scenario needs to be supplemented with a few comments. First, there may be political problems owing to households' resistance to a new system of prices that will require a change in the structure (and, to some extent, in the level) of consumption. These problems must be solved by politicians by means of a restored democratic mechanism. Second, difficulties may arise in finding adequate numbers of responsible worker-entrepreneurs to make company self-management a reality. Third, there will be costs stemming from industrial adjustment. These costs will take the form of closing down some plants and writing off their production assets, as well as temporary unemployment in some branches of industry and localities.

There will be other difficulties, too. A market economy will not eradicate human vices; it will only place a systemic harness on them, preventing them from damaging social organisation. Dishonesty and wrongdoing will continue to exist, perhaps even more painful in the new system than in the old one. Market and competition will not eliminate these transgressions. But the economy as a whole, in its general processes and overall economic dimensions, will develop and generate a growing total of social utility, which will help to relieve individual adversities.

The main condition for a successful transition to a new system is that companies should seek to expand in the pursuit of maximum profit and, equally, that households should seek to obtain higher earnings by increased work efficiency. We have to hope that the forty years of socialism have not entirely destroyed the spirit of industry and innovation in the people. Recent strong growth in private agriculture and the urban private sector bode well in this respect.

Although the above scenario may seem very distant from the present system, which has been suffocating the country for over forty years, certain facts indicate that the vision is not merely an abstract mental speculation. In the Polish social consciousness, profound changes are taking place in the judgement of the existing system, and in the readiness to abandon it and adopt a different system, a different economy. The background for these changes is the growing disbelief that socialism is capable of bringing people wealth, or even a modest well-being, even in return for the loss of individual freedom. Feelings of pessimism about the country's economic prospects, discouragement and reluctance to make efforts, and humiliation at the thought that, right in the middle of Europe, we are not even a third-world but a fourth-world country are spreading more and more. Such attitudes are noticeable even among the establishment, among party and government circles. Gone from official announcements is the self-confidence of old, and what top-level officials say at meetings with workers is infantile and trite. Low spirits among the 'high command' are evinced by the difficulties in agreeing on the 1986 Central Annual Plan and the 1986-90 National Social-Economic Plan. In discussions on the draft versions, so many objections were raised that it would seem simply inconceivable to pass them. The Sejm will undoubtedly pass them nevertheless, but it will be a purely formal act and the documents will be of no consequence for no one is going to believe in them.

All the signs indicate that the time is growing ripe for profound changes in actual economic processes and in the nation's consciousness. Then, the scenario of actions we have suggested may become a useful source of inspiration and instruction.

Comment
by Jacek Rostowski

☆ *Jacek Rostowski is Senior Lecturer in Economics at Kingston Polytechnic and also teaches at the School of Soviet and East European Studies, University of London.*

INTRODUCTORY NOTE

The "second stage of the reform" outlined by Prime Minister Messner on 10 October 1987 which has received so much publicity in the Western media goes a little bit of the way to adopting the proposals put forward in the Report on the Polish Economy printed here. The right noises have been made: the size and powers of the central economic bureaucracy are to be reduced, subsidies to socialised enterprises are to be cut, workers' councils are to receive more power, a securities market is to be created. Although limited compared to those in the Report, the governments proposals are definitely welcome. Unfortunately, all of them were supposed to have been introduced in the first stage of the reform (at that time simply called the economic reform) of 1981-2. They were not introduced because of the power of vested interests in the bureaucracy (the notorious heavy industry lobbies), and the fear of the 'anarchy of the market' which still characterises central decision makers, and to some extent the population as a whole. The authors of the Report believe that the main purpose of the 'second stage' is to remove from the authorities the responsibility for highly unpopular price increases, which the government believes to be unavoidable, and place it on the shoulders of impersonal market forces. Certainly Prime Minister Messner's speech gave credence to such a view.[1] If this is indeed the case, the authorities are likely to be disappointed. The authors of the Report point out that unless the generalised excess demand that characterises the Polish economy is tackled shortages will persist (if centralised price control is maintained), or it will lead to hyperinflation (if price control is abolished).

Nevertheless, it is encouraging to see a Communist Prime Minister state that: "... the role of the state as the organiser of economic life ought to rest upon ... controlling [the legality of undertakings] within ... the universal application of unequivocal rules of the economic game"; that: "... everything that is not forbidden is permitted ..."; and not least that: "The socialised sector ... has become for many people just a place where one acquires the guarantee of employment, permanent payment, social insurance, the right to free health care". Understanding of the problems facing Poland and other communist economies seems to be advancing.[2] More important, and unfortunately less certain, is whether the new understanding will be transformed into effective action.

The group of independent Polish economists who have written this report on the current state of the Polish economic crisis draw attention to two facts above all:
1.   the superficial economic recovery which began in 1982 has effectively come to an end, and this has occurred at a time when the

---

1.   Jacek Rostowski BBC Summary of World Broadcasts, EE/8697/C/3.

2.   Much confusion remains. The speech contains simultaneously the pledge to use the power of the central bureaucracy [sic!] to ensure adequately high differentials for skilled workers, and one not to allow low income families to suffer as a result of the proposed price increases. Private individuals are to have access to the new securities market, yet '... it would be almost entirely a flow of resources between socialised enterprises.' (Nor is it clear why socialised enterprises should wish to lend to each other at all.)

negative effects of the crisis which began in 1979 have not had their full impact on the economy;

2. the policies undertaken to achieve a long-term solution to the crisis are woefully inadequate. From this the authors deduce the immenence of a further economic crisis, which they expect to lead to a political crisis. It is a mark of the bankruptcy of current economic policy in Poland that these independent experts see hope for an improvement in economic policy only in political upheaval. While it may be doubted whether political upheaval is as imminent as the authors of the report believe, and indeed whether a full blown economic crisis of the magnitude of 1979-82 is on the horizon, there can be little doubt that:

(a) the Polish recovery of 1982-4 has run out of steam;
(b) Poland is set for an indefinite period of economic stagnation;
(c) a number of processes are occurring under the surface of economic life which *could* lead to acute economic crisis and social upheaval at any time between now and the end of the century. That the authorities are conscious of this change is indicated by the new reform proposals announced in October 1987.

The report, thanks to its detailed analysis of the chronic elements in Poland's poor economic performance, takes on a wider significance than merely a forecast of what is likely to happen in one particular country. It shows one of the ways in which the worldwide loss of vitality of the socialist economies, which is occurring as the simple 'extensive' reserves of economic growth (underemployed labour, capital and natural resources) are being used up, can manifest itself in a middle-sized, middle-developed European country with a severe debt problem. Prof. Gertrude Shroeder's *The System versus Progress,* published in 1986 by CRCE, discussed the effects of the same underlying loss of vitality on the superpower economy of the USSR. Forthcoming studies to be published by CRCE will analyse the causes and manifestations of this loss of vitality in Hungary, Romania and Yugoslavia, each of which face distinct economic circumstances and have different economic systems.

The situation described in Part III of the report still holds at the end of the first half of 1987. Industrial output grew 3.1% compared with the same period in 1986, construction fell 0.8% and transport of goods (in millions of tons) fell by 4.9%.[1] From this it can be deduced that national income probably rose about 2.5%, or 1.5% per capita. This is a dramatic decline in the rate of growth from the almost 6% achieved in 1983, and reflects what the report calls the 'declining curve' of production. With investment growing faster than consumption, per capita growth in consumption is just about zero. What is more, this will not improve for the foreseeable future. Even the official five year plan for 1986-90 aims for a growth rate of only 3.3% per annum,[2] with consumption growing at 2-3% (i.e. 1-2% on per capita basis), since investment needs to grow faster to offset the 'decapitalisation' (i.e. the depreciation of machines) in Polish industry which is the most important long term effect of the economic crisis. In this context the deterioration in the quality of quite ordinary goods, and the unavailability of consumer durables (leading over time to the 'decapitalization of households') mentioned in the report, take on a new significance. People's true standard of living is probably falling as the quality of goods and the state of durables deteriorates. Although a declining standard of living is not in itself a cause of inevitable economic collapse or social upheaval, it does pose very sharply the question of 'what is to be done' for decision makers. Unfortunately, the argument advanced in the report that under present political conditions the answer will be 'very little', is convincing.

The Polish economy seems locked-in to stagnation for the foreseeable future. One can begin one's description of the vicious circle of powerlessness wherever one wishes, but the conclusion is always the same. The lack of incentives to cut costs under socialism means that the energy intensity of production is exceedingly high. With coal production set to stagnate for the foreseeable future (since the most easily obtained coal has already been extracted) the government is cutting down on home construction which is highly energy intensive. This has driven up both the free market price and the waiting time for flats so far that according to one author of The Report, it has created 'dead ranges' in the marginal utility of money for many people, particularily skilled workers. Most people can effectively buy almost nothing with any additional income they can expect to obtain through additional effort, except for alcohol (which now accounts for 12% of consumer expenditure!). The result is that, in spite of a growing differentiation of income, wages do not act effectively as an incentive. At the same time both price and wage inflation are continuing out of control. This is the result of the political weakness of the authoritiews, which are strong enough to maintain themselves in power but are too weak to take on the workers of large factories on economic issues. The effect is that price inflation has risen to 20%, while 'repressed inflation' (which manifests itself as shortages) is also increasing. Repressed inflation further reduces the effectiveness of money wages as an incentive to better work, while open inflation undermines the authority of the government in economic matters, and makes it hard for enterprises, both socialised and private, to make sensible plans for the future. As the report points out, price inflation is one of the sources of excessive investment demand in the socialised sector. Enterprise managers, unable to maintain the value of financial assets they hold, spend them on inventories and buildings which will cost more later in any case. In the case of buildings this deprives the housing co-operatives of the building materials they need, leading to the 'dead ranges' in the marginal utility of money we mentioned above.

Price and repressed inflation have caused economic and political crisis in Poland in the past. The present situation contains two additional elements which might turn the current stagnation or slow decline in living standards into a collapse: foreign trade and agriculture. After turning a hard-currency trade deficit of $750 million in 1981 into a surplus of $1.4 billion in 1984, Poland has relaxed its efforts, and in 1985 and 1986 ran hard-currency trade surpluses of just over $1 billion, and looks set for much the same result in 1987. Since the interest owed on hard-currency debt is almost $3 billion each yaer and invisible earning amount to somewhat under $1 billion each year, Poland is running a hard-currency balance of payments deficit of about $1 billion each year, which accumulates as increased debt. Net hard-currency debt now stands at about $35 billion, or almost seven times annual hard-currency exports.

The latest revised version of the external adjustment programme (presented to the World Bank in June 1987) sees the debt continuing to grow for the rest of the decade and being stablilized in 1991, two years earlier than previously planned. With much larger debtors such as Brazil in severe trouble with their repayments, there is no danger that Poland will be subjected to a punitive response by the West to its effective default, particularly in the light of its newly acquired good intentions. However, given their record it is legitimate to doubt whether the Polish authorities will persevere with this new policy in the face of mounting shortages on the domestic market. These are already growing rapidly as a result of the somewhat more export oriented stance adopted this year.[3] The danger is therefore that Poland will soon revert to its recent policy of servicing its debt at the lowest level possible. Even that policy required that Poland exported some 20% more lthan it imported in its non-socialist trade. Since non-socialist exports have stagnated for the last four years at about $5.5 billion, with imports at somewhat over $4 billion, everyone agreed that the Polish economy needs more imports from the West if it is to grow. What the Polish authorities did not seem to understand is that for there to be more imports there must first be more exports. Instead they thought of the trade surplus as a tax which has to be grudgingly paid to the West, while being kept as low as possible, so as to maintain access to world markets. The danger is that this policy wil be reverted to in the face of popular dissatisfaction caused by mounting shortages. What is more internal pressure by the population, or a miscalculation by the Polish authorities as to the minimum debt service payments acceptable to the West, could then project the country into formal default, with all the effects on imports and in consequence on domestic production and consumption that such an event will entail

Agriculture has been the most successful branch of the Polish economy since 1982, increasing its gross output by 12.2% by 1986, while inputs into agriculture actually fell, so that net output increased even more (by almost 16%). This success has been due partly to the greater security of property and better prices given to the private peasant farmers who make up the bulk of Polish agriculture, and partly to a run of good weather. Agriculture has also benefited from being more self contained, and thus not suffering as much as other sectors from the shortages which plague the rest of the economy. The success of agriculture has softened the impact of the authorities' inability to control wages (price and repressed inflation were not as great thanks to the increased supply of food), and has also partly offset the country's failure to expand exports of industrial goods. In real terms Poland has cut its non-socialist agricultural import bill by half and increased non-socialist agricultural exports threefold since 1982. The overall effect was to save Poland some $530 million last year. The authors of the report do not believe that this success can continue. For agriculture to continue expanding it has to become more dependent on the rest of the economy for industrial inputs such as pesticides, fertilizers and tractors. Yet the authorities are not prepared to increase the share of industry working for agriculture, nor to end the current supply policy by which the resource wasting state sector of agriculture is favoured. Even more serious are the likely effects of repressed and open inflation on agriculture: how long are farmers likely to work to obtain zlotys with which they cannot obtain the goods they want (what the report calls 'empty zlotys'), and which there is little point in saving with price inflation running at 20%? But if the farmers cease expanding production there will be fewer additional goods, and repressed inflation will get worse, which could set up a vicious circle of declining production.

It is the knowledge that a sharp increase in excess demand must be avoided, coupled with a fear of antagonising the working class through the price increases which it knows to be necessary, which has induced the government to relaunch its economic reform programme under the title of the 'second stage of the reform'. The proposed reforms were outlined in somewhat more detail in mid-October 1987. The report's analysis of the authorities' motives on launching the second stage are convincing: the government hopes to 'depoliticise' the setting of wages and prices by handing these over to autonomous market forces, hoping that it can thus avoid the blame for the reductions in real wages which it knows to be necessary. One of the most interesting parts of the report is its analysis of the internal contradictions of the authorities' reform proposals, and indeed of any attempt to increase the role of markets in a socialist economy without truly radical changes (which would have to go further than the changes introduced so far in Yugoslavia, let alone Hungary!). The first problem is that consumer price increases only reduce demand in these economies, they do not stimulate supply, as they do under capitalism, because of the monopolistic structure of industry, the complete absence of free entry, and fixed prices and shortages on intermediate goods markets which make it impossible to increase output even if one so wishes. The second problem is that the introduction of bankruptcy for unprofitable firms (the so-called 'hardfinancing' we hear so much about from Gorbachev's reformist camp in the Soviet Union) is likely to be counter-productive if prices are fixed. Generalised excess demand in socialist countries means that bankrupting a firm is likely to increase shortages as the firm ceases to operate. The absence of capital markets and the slowness of bureaucratic procedures means it will be a long time before the capital resources freed by bankrupting the firm are put to new uses. In any case, with state fixed prices it is unclear whether loss makers are truly inefficient or merely have a disadvantageous ratio of (state fixed) input prices to output prices. As a result, hardfinancing with fixed prices is likely to lead to a lot of, often unnecessary, structural unemployment. The problem could be solved by allowing enterprises to set their own prices, but in the presence of generalised excess demand this would soon lead to hyperinflation. Abolishing generalised excess demand is therefore what is really necessary, but one cannot avoid the fact that this is certain to lead to, possibly widespread, unemployment as the economy reacts to its liberation from forty years of distorted growth.

Particularly interesting is the view of the authors that under the impact of poor economic performance there have been important changes in social conciousness in Poland in what one might call an 'anti-socialist' direction. Pessimism regarding the economic future under the current system is growing rapidly, and the belief in the superiority of capitalism over socialism and in the greater efficiency of private sector activity in Poland[4] seems to be widespread. According to the report, these beliefs have penetrated the ruling establishment. It is on the basis of this view that the authors suggest that the time is ripe for a truly radical reform which would depend on:

1.   freeing all prices while controlling the growth of households' global purchasing power (presumably through some sort of monetary policy);
2.   handing over the management of enterprises completely to workers' councils so as to ensure enterprise independence of central planners;
3.   an end to cross subsidisation between enterprises;
4.   truly free foreign trade based on a convertible currency.

The authors accept that households are likely to resist the new structure of prices and wages which will result from the free play of market forces. They accept that it is probable that there are not enough 'workers entrepreneurs' to man the workers' councils, and that the emergence of structural unemployment could be a serious political problem. It is here that we come to the weakest part of the report. The authors have little to propose by way of solution to these problems other than the restoration of democratic mechanisms which, they suppose, would enable politicians to resolve these questions. Such a 'solution' seems quite unconvincing. One would be more impressed if the report stated baldly that unemployment for some and sharp reductions in real wages for most people will have to occur, and that this is the price that Poland has to pay now if it is not to pay a greater price later. Unfortunately, it seems that a degree of wishful thinking is common to both independent circles and the authorities in Poland.

Another weakness of the report's proposed radical reform measures is their reliance on workers' control as the basic form of organisation of Polish industry, when the weakness of this form is well known from the Yugoslav experience. Workers' control grafted onto a highly monopolised industrial structure and a highly interventionist state (a habit which is unlikely to be lost overnight), leads to large scale long term structural unemployment and hyperinflation. The alternative, which is simply privatisation, if necessary through 'give aways' of enterprises to workers in cases in which no other buyers can be found, may lead to the same problem of unemployment in the short run, but should be less inflationary from the start, and with time the unemployment also should be absorbed. It is clear that no significant constituency exists in Poland at present for such an economic revolution (such a change could hardly be called merely a reform). The opposition to the Communist government comes mainly from industrial workers, who while they desire to have a decisive say in the running of their own factories, and would be delighted to see them freed from the shackles imposed by central planners, are not likely to support the idea of their privatisation – at least not until they have experienced for a number of years the disadvantages of workers' self-management.[5]

And there is, of course, Poland's geo-political situation, which makes a counter-revolution of the sort suggested here quite impossible at present. It is therefore not surprising that the report does not call for true systemic change in Poland. Still, it has laid down in its proposed reform measures most, though not all, of the fundamental changes which are necessary if Poland is to avoid stagnation or economic collapse and is to resume the path of economic growth. Certainly, the proposals go far further than anything implemented by any socialist country including Yugoslavia, and are far ahead of anything being considered in the Soviet Union. Unfortunately it seems unlikely that the Polish authorities will take advantage of the modest changes being introduced in the Soviet Union to push on further by introducing reforms on the lines proposed in the report.

FOOTNOTES

1. Plan fulfillment report for the first six months of 1987 in *Zycie Gospodarcze*, 25.7.1987.

2. *1986-1990 Five Year Plan* figures provided in *IMF Staff Report on Poland* of September 15 1986.

3. Plan fulfillment report for the first seven months of 1987 in *Zycie Gospodarcze*, 30.8.1987.

4. For instance in 'na recznym hamulcu' by Col. S. Kwiatkowski in *Polityka* 21.3.1987 and 'Dlaczego Kapitalizm nie upada' by D. Passent in *Polityka* 18.7.1987

5. For the disaffection of ordinary workers with self-management see L. Sirc *The Yugoslav Economy Under Self-Management*, MacMillan, London, 1979.

INITIAL RESEARCH PROGRAMME OF THE CENTRE

The broad aim of research is to illuminate the following issues:

1) The crisis of the communist systems and its reasons;

2) changes and policies required to reform these systems and make them more efficient;

3) difficulties communist countries are experiencing in their foreign trade and possible remedies;

4) ways and means of educating the public in communist countries on the need for reform.

The current address of the CRCE is c/o 2 Lord North Street, London SW1P 3LB (tel. 01-799 3745).

The Director can usually be contacted at 41A Westbourne Gardens, Glasgow G12 9XQ.

ISBN 0 948027 08 8

Forthcoming Publications

Does Market Socialism Work?
by Professor Alfred Schuller, University of Marburg
with a comment by Bela Csikos-Nagy,
President, Hungarian Economic Association, Budapest

Spontaneous Order
by Professor Friedrich Hayek, University of Freiburg,
selected and introduced by Dr. Naomi Moldofsky, University of Melbourne,
comments by Dr. Milowit Kuninski, University of Cracow,
and Dr. Sudha Shenoy, University of New South Wales

Publications Planned

Alan Smith, SSEES – on the economic prospects of Rumania
Two Polish economists – on the poverty of communism
An East-European sociologist – on liberation theology
Western and Eastern Philosophers – on the philosophy of the market
Vietnamese and Cambodian economists – on economics and politics of Indochina
Jacek Rostowski, Kingston Polytechnic – on pollution under socialism
Ljubo Sirc, Director CRCE – on the IMF advice to Yugoslavia
Professor Silvana Malle, University of Verona – on planning and markets in Soviet labour allocation

Previously Published

Market or Plan?
by Professor Milton Friedman, Hoover Institution, Stanford,
and Professor Alec Nove, Glasgow University
ISBN 0 948027 00 2 £2.00

Marxian Utopia?
by Dr. Neven Sesardic, University of Zagreb,
and Professor Domenico Settembrini, University of Pisa
ISBN 0 948027 01 0 £3.50

How Social is the Market Economy?
by Professor Walter Wittmann, University of Fribourg
ISBN 0 948027 02 9 £2.50

The Enemies of the People
by Kosta Cavoski, Belgrade Institute of Comparative Law
ISBN 0 948027 03 7 £3.50

Stagnation or Change in Communist Economies?
by Professor Karl C. Thalheim, Berlin, and
Professor Gregory Grossman, Berkeley
ISBN 0 948027 04 5 £3.50

The System versus Progress
Soviet Economic Problems by Professor Gertrude Schroeder, University of Virginia,
Introduced by Dr. Phil Hanson, University of Birmingham
ISBN 0 948027 05 3 £3.50

Economic Prospects – East and West
A view from the East
Jan Winiecki, University of Lublin
Comment: Roger Clarke, Institute of Soviet and East European Studies, Glasgow
ISBN 0 948027 06 1 £5.00

80464
54